BERLIN

Jack Altman

G000166031

JPMGUIDES

Contents

Right: Köpenick town hall

This Way Berlin

United but Changing

This is not a town you can pin down. You can never say at any one time what Berlin *is*, only what it's *becoming*. Germany's capital offers constantly stimulating reminders of the unstable soil of swamp and sand into which it has sunk its foundations. Berliners are used to seeing their buildings knocked down, by war, by imperial and communist despots or capitalist speculators, then resurrected or replaced by something equally grandiose, outrageous or, at times, just banal. Look away for a moment and everything changes: now it's the capital, now it isn't, now half is the capital of a truncated country, the German Democratic Republic (GDR or East Germany), and half—on the other side of the infamous Wall—is a beleaguered Western frontier town in the Cold War. Today, after seeing both the Wall and the GDR, Berlin has entered the 21st century, once more the proud capital of a whole country.

Focus Shifts East

The town is jumping. The construction boom of the 1990s has not let up. The vast Potsdamer Platz, a bleak wasteland throughout the years of the Wall, has returned to being a throbbing centre for entertainment and commerce, with new theatres, hotels, cafés, bars, restaurants and a pleasant shopping mall. To meet the transfer of government and its bureaucracy from Bonn, the venerable Reichstag parliament has been gutted and renovated, new ministries and embassies built, and others reclaimed. Superb art collections split up during 50 years of the Cold War have been reunited in new museums, while old ones have been restored after decades of neglect. Churches have been rescued from their communist conversion to discotheques—the latter happily moving on to disused breweries and other more appropriately congenial premises.

Historically, Berlin has always had more than one "centre". In 1920, the creation of Greater Berlin united 8 towns, 29 rural communes and 27 independent districts. Today, of all the many changes, one of the most remarkable has been the revival of eastern Berlin. After years of being dismissed as dreary and characterless, with at most the curiosity value of a Stalinist stronghold, the "east" has seen its neighbourhoods of Mitte, Friedrichshain and Prenzlauer Berg thrive again with boutiques, art galleries and restaurants. It is regaining something of the vibrant atmosphere it enjoyed in Berlin's Golden Twenties.

The Kurfürstendamm, Western Berlin's glitzy boulevard, the smart side streets of Charlottenburg and chic Savignyplatz now face competition from the new and refurbished buildings on Unter den Linden, Friedrichstrasse and the less flashy but increasingly lively area around Kollwitzplatz in the east. Even the gigantic apartment buildings on Karl-Marx-Allee that served as a showcase for bombastic Stalinist architecture in the 1950s have had their façades spruced up.

Not all is new. Many of the finer Prussian monuments of the 18th century still stand: the Hohenzollern monarchs' summer residence, Schloss Charlottenburg, the Brandenburg Gate leading to Friedrich the Great's edifices on Unter den Linden, the elegant Gendarmenmarkt's French and German cathedrals flanking the Konzerthaus. And not all is charming. Hitler's Olympic Stadium has survived (though it will be transformed for the 2006 World Cup), as have the Nazis' bleak and soulless office buildings on Leipziger Strasse, Fehrbelliner Platz and Platz der Luftbrücke (at Tempelhof airport).

Theatre, Music and Cabaret

Berlin is once more at the centre of the country's cultural scene. Performing in the acoustically magnificent Philharmonie concert hall, the Berlin Philharmonic remains one of the world's greatest orchestras. Germany's leading actors and an enthusiastic public are drawn to plays at the revived Berliner Ensemble created by Bertolt Brecht, the innovative Schaubühne, and the energetic Deutsches Theater founded by Max Reinhardt. And the city's famous summer Love Parade brings young ravers from all over Europe and beyond.

Germany is not famous for its sense of humour. Berlin is. This is quite an achievement, considering the stiff and starchy Prussians who historically made up the city's ruling class. The *Berliner Schnauze* (Berlin lip) has always been

Give him three pennies,
he may play you an opera.

part of the turbulent city's survival kit. In the 1920s, its citizens' sardonic wit made itself most keenly felt in the satirical cabarets. If Hitler disliked Berlin so much, the people's humour was certainly partly to blame. Taxi drivers, street vendors and bartenders are as mordant as ever. After a long period in the doldrums, the cabarets have bounced back, relishing in particular the arrival of the federal government with its inevitable scandals and power struggles.

In the Cold War years the city benefited from an influx of West German students and young artists attracted by the Bonn government's offer of subsidies and exemption from military service. This placed Berlin, always young at heart, in the vanguard of Germany's counter-culture known here as the "alternative scene". After the fall of the Wall, the most creative elements spread out from their base in working-class Kreuzberg to the eastern borough of Prenzlauer Berg.

Melting pot

With a population of about 3.4 million, Berlin is a sprawling metropolis of 890 sq km (344 sq miles) and, like London, a city of boroughs, many of them veritable villages. The city is delightfully green and airy. Lakes, forests and parks cover over a third of the metropolitan area. The sandy soil provides excellent bathing beaches along the Havel River and the lake shores of the Wannsee and Müggelsee—ideal for sailing. Berlin is flat, but the rubble of Allied bombardments in World War II was used to form artificial hills: the Teufelsberg in Grunewald or Mont Klamott in Friedrichshain, providing good viewpoints and acceptable ski slopes in the winter. Southwest of the capital is the old Prussian royal court city of Potsdam, easiest of leisurely day trips.

The end of the Cold War also restored to Berlin its pivotal role in relations between eastern and western Europe. A glance at the telephone book reveals the quantity of Slavonic names. Poles, Russians and citizens of many of the old Soviet republics are a fixture of the Berlin scene. Notably, the arrival of Jews from these countries has increased their community, numbering only a few hundred survivors after World War II, to over 12,000. Municipal statistics set the population of Polish origin at 29,000. The largest "foreign" community is Turkish, some 160,000 strong, while the former Yugoslavia claims more than 76,000, Italy 12,000 and Greece 11,000.

Flashback

First Things First

Signs of people living in the area date back over 10,000 years, but it was not until well into the Middle Ages—the municipality's modern name was first mentioned in 1244—that anybody could honestly say *"Ich bin ein Berliner"*. For most of its history, the city as we know it now was a cluster of highly independent-minded villages founded to exploit the fishing and trading facilities of the Havel and Spree rivers and surrounding lakes. In fact, some of them, like Charlottenburg, Wilmersdorf, Schöneberg, Köpenick and Spandau did not become part of Berlin until 1920. Those Stone Age nomads left flint weapons and a few reindeer bones, but the first real settlers, around 3000 BC, were probably farmers.

An early Germanic tribe moved into the southwest district of Teltow in the 6th century BC. In the 6th century AD, colonies of Slavonic Sorbs began settling in Köpenick on the Spree River and Spandau on the Havel.

Middle Ages

The thriving Slav communities of farmers and craftsmen—skilled weavers, potters and carpenters—were in turn absorbed by tough migrant German merchants in the 12th century. They came from the Rhineland, Westphalia and Saxony, followed later by others from Thuringia. From the Ascanian dynasty in the Harz Mountains, Albrecht the Bear provided Berlin's future emblem, ruling the surrounding state of Brandenburg as its first margrave (1157–70).

It was only in the 13th century that the city began to take shape in the loose association of its component communities. Cölln was a fishing village (now Fischerinsel) on an island in the Spree. The Mühlendamm embankment linked it to the township of Berlin on the north bank, where travelling salesmen found hospitable inns and rental carts for their merchandise. Its marketplace around the church of St Nicholas has been reconstructed as the quaint Nikolaiviertel tourist area.

Berlin and Cölln joined forces in 1307 to combat bands of highway robbers upsetting their trade with Poland. They built a joint town hall on a bridge between the two townships, with two councils governing in tandem. The system

worked well enough for them to join, in 1359, the prosperous Hanseatic League of cities trading from the North Sea and the Baltic.

Hohenzollerns Move In

In the 15th century, Hohenzollern princes from south Germany took over Brandenburg. They made their home in Berlin-Cölln and cut back the dual township's municipal autonomy.

During the Reformation, the Berliners re-asserted their independent spirit by forcing Prince-Elector Joachim II to embrace the Protestant creed of Martin Luther in 1539. Their motivation was not so much religious as practical, but nonetheless high-minded. The money they saved on Catholic church taxes served to turn a monastery into a printing press and publishing house and to found a secular high school (*Gymnasium*) next door.

The Thirty Years' War (1618–48) gave no reason to be high-minded about religion. The city was laid waste first by the Swedish troops of Gustavus Adolphus, who championed the Protestant cause, and then

Irony of history, parts of the infamous Wall are now protected monuments.

by the Catholic army of the German Emperor. Plague, famine and war cut the population in half, from 12,000 to 6,000.

Capital of Prussia

The city began to take on the appearance of a real capital under Friedrich-Wilhelm, the Great Elector (1640–88). He added fortifications, planted trees from his castle to the Tiergarten along the avenue that was to become Unter den Linden, and above all took drastic measures to increase the population. In 1671, he welcomed some 50 wealthy Jewish refugee families from Vienna. They were followed by nearly 6,000 Protestant Huguenots driven from France after Louis XIV revoked the Edict of Nantes. Later, other Protestants joined them, coming from Switzerland and the Rhineland Palatinate. These newcomers—many of them sophisticated merchants, jewellers, tailors of high fashion, gourmet chefs—brought a refined, cosmopolitan flavour that was rare in other German cities of the day. By 1700, the population numbered over 50,000.

The Great Elector's son inherited both Brandenburg and the eastern German territories of Prussia in 1688. Since the latter also included Polish lands, in 1701 he crowned himself King Friedrich I *in* but not *of* Prussia. He let his energetic wife Sophie Charlotte guide him in founding Berlin's academies for the arts and sciences and commissioning great baroque architects like Andreas Schlüter. The royal palace, the Berliner Schloss, was destroyed in 1951, but other buildings on Unter den Linden and the queen's summer palace, Charlottenburg, testify to this first flowering of Prussian splendour.

Their frugal son Friedrich-Wilhelm I (1713–40) cultivated a new and more rigid spirit of *Preussentum* (Prussianness). He preferred beer to wine, the barracks to the palace. After his coronation, the Sergeant King, as he was nicknamed, sold off his robes and the royal silver to pay off his extravagant parents' debts, and ordered his courtiers to dress in military uniform. He turned the royal pleasure-garden (still known as the *Lustgarten*) into a parade ground, and in his mother's gardens at Charlottenburg planted cabbages in place of flowers.

Friedrich II (1740–86) duly rebelled against the stuffy philistine legacy of his father's court. He practically abandoned Berlin to devote himself to creating in Potsdam an elegant but more intimate version of Louis XIV's Versailles. The language at his Sanssouci Palace was French, and Voltaire was its honoured resident philosopher. A writer and musician, the king also proved himself a much more brilliant soldier than the Sergeant King —always contemptuous of his son's "effete" manners—ever imagined possible. His victories in Silesia in 1745 earned him the title of Friedrich der Grosse (Frederick the Great), King of and not just *in* Prussia.

Berlin itself did benefit from Prussia's grandeur as a capital of the Enlightenment, with Friedrich adding to Unter den Linden the grand opera house (*Deutsche Staatsoper*), buildings that are now part of Humboldt University, and above all the Brandenburg Gate, begun just after his death.

Uniting the German Nation

Napoleon's humiliating victory over the Prussian armies in 1806, underlined by his arrogant entry into Berlin through the Brandenburg Gate, stoked the fires of a new patriotism after the French were driven out of Germany in 1813. Authoritarian Prussia was worried by the nationalist movement's demands for a constitutional monarchy and freedom of the press. These subversive ideas rapidly spread through Berlin's university, founded in 1810, and *Lesecafés* (reading cafés), where intellectuals found in foreign periodicals the news denied them by the capital's strict press censorship.

Unease grew in high places as the new proletariat created by the Industrial Revolution doubled the city's population to more than 400,000 in the first half of the 19th century. In 1848, workers demonstrated at the palace against factory and living conditions. The Prussian cavalry opened fire and killed 230. After granting concessions to liberal demands, the government went on to increase press censorship and police repression of political meetings. Workers' housing was scarcely improved by the grim tenements known as *Mietskasernen* (rent barracks) that first appeared in 1862.

That same year, Otto von Bismarck became Prussia's Iron Chancellor and set about appropriating the German nationalist movement for his king Wilhelm I. After decisive Prussian-led victories over Austria and France, Wilhelm was proclaimed Kaiser (Emperor) of the German Reich in 1871, and Berlin became its increasingly prosperous capital. It was the era of department stores and mass-circulation newspapers. Following the route of the new railway linking Berlin to Potsdam, the entrepreneurial bourgeoisie erected its villas around the Wannsee lake and the Grunewald forest southwest of the capital. Bismarck had the Kurfürstendamm built to emulate Paris's Champs-Elysées. But the boom of the Reich's *Gründerzeit* (Founding Years) also led many to financial ruin and caused mass unemployment.

To counter the rampant materialism of these early years as the political capital, Berlin began to assert its cultural status. The arrival of Viennese director Max Reinhardt at the head of the Deutsches Theater in 1905 inspired it to become the top theatre city in Europe. Tchaikovsky, Richard Strauss and Grieg worked as guest composers for the Berlin Philharmonic. Artists Max Liebermann, Max Slevogt and Lovis Corinth contested Munich's leadership in German painting. In the sciences, winning Nobel prizes was a local sport—Robert Koch was awarded his for discovering the tuberculosis bacillus, Max Planck and Albert Einstein for their work in physics. It was said that of the ten people who understood Einstein's theory of relativity, eight lived in Berlin.

War and the Republic

World War I began in euphoria, with crowds cheering Kaiser Wilhelm II on the balcony of the Berliner Schloss. The grim realities of food rationing and thousands killed on the western front soon turned popular feeling against the war. The Spartacus League of Rosa Luxemburg and Karl Liebknecht, the precursor of the German Communist Party, organized worker opposition which culminated in a strike of 400,000 Berlin workers in January 1918.

By November, returning soldiers had joined workers to fly the red flag of revolution, riding through the streets with machine guns mounted on their trucks. But the political left was split. On November 9, Liebknecht stood on the balcony of the Berliner Schloss, with the crowds this time cheering the proclamation of a Soviet-style socialist republic. That same day, the anti-Bolshevik Social Democrats (SPD) had already gathered at the Reichstag to proclaim a German Republic—and they held the reins of governmental power. Chancellor Friedrich Ebert let his defence minister Gustav Noske call in 4,000 right-wing *Freikorps* militia to crush the Spartacists. The storm troopers assassinated Liebknecht and Luxemburg on January 15, 1919, just four days before parliamentary elections. To escape the turmoil of the capital, Reichstag deputies moved temporarily to Weimar to vote the constitution for the new republic.

The "Golden" Twenties

Governing the Weimar Republic in Germany's first shaky experience of parliamentary democracy, Berlin presented a stage that was both frightening and exhilarating. The SPD's use of the Freikorps to defeat their rivals set an example for the right-wing Kapp Putsch of March 1920. The attempt by 5,000 storm-troopers to impose a civil servant, Wolfgang Kapp, as puppet chancellor lasted only five days, but their helmets provided a significantly more enduring emblem: the swastika adopted by Adolf Hitler's Nazis. Political assassination became commonplace. Notably in 1922, foreign minister Walther Rathenau, a cultivated liberal Jewish industralist, was shot dead in a street near the Grunewald. The struggle to redress defeated Germany's position in the international arena was waged against a background of economic crisis. Bankruptcies and crippling inflation beset Berlin just as it was incor-

A former checkpoint over the Spree, the beautiful Oberbaum Bridge linking the Kreuzberg and Friedrichshain districts was restored in the 1990s.

porating into one metropolis scores of suburban villages and hitherto autonomous townships like Spandau, Köpenick and Charlottenburg, doubling the city's population to nearly 4 million.

The turbulence marking the new-found democratic freedoms also proved enormously creative. Wilhelm Furtwängler reigned at the Berlin Philharmonic, and Bruno Walter, Otto Klemperer and Erich Kleiber at the Opera. From 1919 to 1932, the city staged world premieres of 12 major new operas. Culturally, 1920s Berlin was the most exciting city in Europe. And the craziest, too. The paintings of Otto Dix, Max Beckmann and George Grosz, and the brutal photomontages of John Heartfield mirrored the harsh realities of the times. But as a Dada-ist forerunner of the Surrealists, Grosz might also be seen staging with writer Walter Mehring a race between a typewriter and a sewing machine. Nightclubs served up whisky and cocaine, striptease and ferocious political satire. In the theatre, Reinhardt's grandiose commercial productions gave way to the revolutionary dramas of Erwin Piscator and Bertolt Brecht, accompanied by the acerbic music of Kurt Weill. Josef von Sternberg's film *The Blue Angel* symbolized the changing Prussian image with the seduction of the professor (Ernst Jannings) by the cabaret singer (Marlene Dietrich). Berlin cinema was at its height, and Hollywood could scarcely wait to get its hands on directors like Fritz Lang and Ernst Lubitsch.

Hitler made it all possible. In 1926, he sent propagandist Joseph Goebbels to direct operations in Berlin, where Nazis and Communists fought bloody street battles. The Nazis gained the upper hand by exploiting divisions among their opponents, and artists and writers, Jewish and otherwise, fled the capital.

The Third Reich

On January 31, 1933, President Hindenburg's duly democratic appointment of Adolf Hitler as German chancellor was celebrated by a torchlit parade of Nazi storm troopers through the Brandenburg Gate. A fire in the Reichstag a month later gave Hitler the pretext he needed to impose a tyranny of terror. The Dutch communist arrested on the spot claimed that he was working alone, and a communist plot was never proved, but the Gestapo

secret police nonetheless proceeded to crush all political opposition. Communists and Social Democrats were sent to the newly opened concentration camps, of which Oranienburg, just outside Berlin, was one of the first.

In May 1933, Nazi students marched along Unter den Linden to their university to burn books of Jewish, humanist and other subversive authors. Jews were systematically excluded from public life. During the triumph of Berlin's 1936 Olympic Games, "*Juden unerwünscht*" ("Jews undesirable") signs vanished from cafés, hotels and shops until foreign visitors left town. (The Olympic Stadium still stands.)

Any international illusions about the fate of the Jews ought to have been dispelled on November 9, 1938, when the Nazis spurred on crowds to burn synagogues and smash and loot Jewish-owned shops all over the country. *Kristallnacht* (Crystal Night), as the event became known, earned its name from the broken glass of a huge chandelier in Berlin's Wertheim department store. Just over three years later, in an elegant Wannsee villa, Adolf Eichmann received instructions at a ministerial conference to organize the "Final Solution of the European Jewish Question". Berlin's Jewish population was reduced by extermination and emigration from 160,564 in 1933 to 7,272 in 1945. (After the creation of the state of Israel, only a few hundred remained, until immigrants from the former Soviet Union brought the number back up in recent times to some 12,000.)

A furious Hitler could not understand why, unlike in 1914, Berliners did not cheer the 1939 mobilization for World War II. In retaliation for the London Blitz, British bombardments in August 1940 quickly brought the war to the home front. By 1945, Anglo-American air raids and Soviet ground shelling had reduced much of the city to rubble. On April 30, as Soviet troops advanced through the streets, Hitler committed suicide in his bunker below Wilhelmstrasse.

Split by the Cold War

Situated entirely within Soviet-occupied East Germany, Berlin came under four-power control after the wartime Allies' Potsdam Conference of 1945. The Soviet-controlled eastern sector covered almost half the city's total area, while American, British and French sectors soon came together as West Berlin. This truncated capitalist metropolis was a constant thorn in the flesh of Moscow's communist regime. The 1948 Soviet blockade of road, rail and waterway links to West Germany was broken by American and British planes airlifting daily supplies of food and industrial equipment. East Berlin was proclaimed capital of the new German Democratic Republic in 1949, with veteran Stalinist Walter Ulbricht as its leader, while West Berlin became a rather garish showcase for Western democracy.

In 1953, an uprising by East German workers against Stalinist repression and wretched living conditions was crushed by Soviet tanks. Protest continued with the flight of nearly 3 million East Germans to the West by 1960. The loss of highly qualified engineers, doctors and skilled workers was costing the GDR millions of marks invested in their training. Soviet leader Nikita Khrushchev instructed Ulbricht to stop the haemorrhage by closing the East-West Berlin border. The massive Wall that grew out of this border closure became a symbol of the Cold War, both of the bankruptcy of the communist system and the Western democracies' cynical acquiescence in the status quo.

Only foreigners and West Germans could cross into East Berlin at special checkpoints.

West Berliners had to wait till their former mayor, Chancellor Willy Brandt, broke the Cold War ice in the 1970s. In hindsight, his *Ostpolitik* (Eastern Policy) of forging links with the Soviet bloc was an essential step in bringing down the Wall itself.

Bringing It All Together Again

Erich Honecker succeeded Ulbricht in 1971. He made a vain effort to stay afloat by artificially pumping up a woefully inefficient and corrupt economy, leaving the GDR as grotesquely bloated as its muscle-bound Olympic athletes. The East Berliners' new television sets only served to show that they could get much better cars, refrigerators and stereo equipment on the other side of the Wall. From 1987 to summer 1989, a new wave of refugees made its way to the West via Poland, Czechoslovakia and Hungary. After Soviet leader Mikhail Gorbachev came to Berlin in October 1989 and let it be known that Soviet tanks would no longer protect the GDR, Honecker resigned, soon followed by his government. The Wall fell on November 9. The harbinger of the collapse of international communism, Berlin was once again at the centre of world history.

Striking while the iron was hot, Chancellor Helmut Kohl pushed quickly for reunification. It was celebrated at the Reichstag on October 3, 1990, and Berlin was once again proclaimed the nation's capital. Nine years later, a Social Democratic chancellor, Gerhard Schroeder, ushered in the government move from Bonn to Berlin.

As people concentrated on the building boom, with ministries, embassies, office blocks and new housing shooting up all over the city, a problem still remained of integrating east and west Berliners. For many, the Wall may have gone, but the social, economic and psychological differences of 45 years of separation are still a reality. Others see a positive sign in the fact that eastern Berlin's Mitte and Prenzlauer Berg, for so long the "poor relations" among the city's neighbourhoods, have become fashionable places in which to live and have fun. Now, the east is "in".

Today, the city that seemed condemned to remain a provincial backwater in its Cold War years is once more a vibrant, cosmopolitan, cultural capital. Weimar and Bonn are distant memories. Germany has entered the era of the Berlin Republic.

Sightseeing

Germany's new capital is huge. You can get around quickly by underground or overhead trains, or by hopping onto a bus or tram. To save you some legwork we have grouped the sights by district, starting at the centre with the Brandenburg Gate.

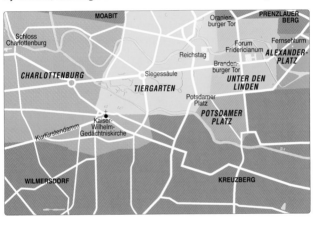

UNTER DEN LINDEN

East of the Brandeburg Gate lies Mitte (Middle), Berlin's historic centre. Its prestigious avenue, Unter den Linden, is lined with banks, ministries and luxury hotels. About halfway along, the avenue is bisected by Friedrichstrasse, a vital north-south thoroughfare. To the north, around Oranienburger Strasse, is the old Jewish quarter.

Brandenburg Gate F 2*

At the entrance to Berlin's royal avenue, Unter den Linden, this grandiose monument carries on its broad neoclassical shoulders the full symbolic weight of the city's history. Completed in 1793, Carl Gotthard Langhans' design was inspired by the gatehouse to the Parthenon in Athens. The Doric columns are flanked by what were originally a Prussian Army guard-house and a tollbooth for collecting customs duties.

On top of the gate, Johann Gottfried Schadow's bronze Quadriga—Winged Victory driving a chariot pulled by four horses—was intended by the sculptor to symbolize peace, as depicted by the procession he carved beneath it in sandstone, and if his wish had been granted the gate would have been called Friedenstor (Gate of Peace). But the Prussian kings saw it as a monument to celebrate their wars, for which they commissioned the gate's other friezes.

Napoleon led his victorious army through the gate, as did his conqueror at Waterloo, Field Marshall Blücher. Other marches here demonstrated for freedom—against the Prussian monarchy in 1848 and against the Stalinist regime in 1953—but also for tyranny, with the Nazi torchlight parade of 1933.

The gate towered over the divided city when the Wall was built across it in 1966 and became the focus of reunification when the Wall came down in 1989.

Pariser Platz F 2

Reduced to rubble in World War II, the square immediately east of the Brandenburg Gate is assuming once more its role of "drawing room" *(Salon)* for the grand Unter den Linden avenue, its trees replanted and many buildings restored.

Framing the gate, two sandstone mansions have been rebuilt in their patrician 19th-century style: to the

---

*References correspond to the fold-out map at the end of the guide.

eft (north), the Max-Liebermann-Haus, where the Impressionist painter lived for 40 years; to the right, its twin, Haus Sommer. On the square's southeast corner, the monumental Hotel Adlon has re-opened to welcome well-heeled guests. They have a hard act to follow: the Rockefellers, Lawrence of Arabia, Albert Einstein, Charlie Chaplin and Enrico Caruso. The Akademie der Künste (Fine Arts Academy), the French embassy, bank and office buildings have arisen on their original sites; the American embassy is still undergoing reconstruction.

Unter den Linden F 2

Now that some of its finest historical buildings have been refurbished, this grand avenue is recapturing some of the grandeur of its Prussian heyday. It began in 1573 as a bridle path for the Hohenzollern princes and courtiers riding to the Tiergarten hunting grounds from the Berliner Schloss (the royal palace damaged in World War II and dismantled by the East German regime in 1950).

The avenue's name derived from the lime or linden trees added later to provide shade. It was the only thoroughfare in Berlin that really

SHOPPING AND SHOWS

Since the city's reunification, **Friedrichstrasse** (F 1–G 4) has taken on a dazzling new character. It had always been, from the mid-19th century on, the town's busiest shopping, café and theatre street, but also the sleaziest. Today, it has been rebuilt, like Potsdamer Platz, by the world's top architects, with the city's smartest boutiques, shopping arcades, luxury hotels and fine restaurants. Appropriately at the corner of Französische Strasse (F–G 2), Jean Nouvel designed the sparkling **Galeries Lafayette**, a local branch of the Paris department store which attracts Berliners in equal numbers to its high fashion and gourmet food counters. Just to the south is the equally spectacular but undergound shopping centre, **Friedrichstadt-Passagen**, an opulent design of New York's Henry Cobb, partner to I.M.Pei.

The Friedrichstrasse area has four prominent theatres. On the north bank of the Spree on Schiffbauerdamm is the **Berliner Ensemble**, created by Bertolt Brecht, whose square is nearby. A short walk to the northwest, along Albrechtstrasse, is the **Deutsches Theater** founded by Max Reinhardt, and the **Kammerspielen**. Back on Friedrichstrasse is the bold and brassy **FriedrichstadtPalast** variety hall.

Architectural and religious harmony on elegant Gendarmenmarkt.

interested Friedrich the Great; he laid out his "Forum Fridericianum" halfway down, with buildings that now form part of Humboldt University. At the avenue's western end, near Pariser Platz, is the Russian Embassy, a characteristic Soviet monument completed in 1953, year of Joseph Stalin's death.

Gendarmenmarkt G 3

Turn south down Charlottenstrasse to reach this square, for many the city's most graceful architectural ensemble. It was laid out at the beginning of the 18th century for twin baroque cathedrals commissioned by Friedrich I. On the north side of the square, the Französische Dom (1701) was a gift to Huguenot Protestants who had fled Louis XIV's France in 1685, while German Protestants were given the Deutsche Dom (1708). Both cathedrals are now museums, the French for the Huguenots and the Germans for a permanent exhibition, *Fragen an die deutsche Geschichte* (German History In Question).

Completing the group on the west side is a splendid neoclassical theatre, the Schauspielhaus, built by Karl Friedrich Schinkel in 1821.

Typically, it was Sergeant King Friedrich-Wilhelm I who earned the square its military name by garrisoning a regiment of guards here.

St Hedwigskathedrale G 2
U-Bahn Hausvogteiplatz
Bus 100, 147, 157, 257
Bebelplatz
Tel. 203 48 10
Mon–Sat 10 a.m.–5 p.m.;
Sun 1–5 p.m.

Northeast of Gendarmenmarkt, the broad-domed Catholic St Hedwig's cathedral was built by Friedrich the Great after 10,000 Catholics came to predominantly Protestant Berlin following the Prussian conquest of Silesia in 1745. It was not finished until 1773.

Staatsoper G 2
U-Bahn Hausvogteiplatz
U-, S-Bahn Friedrichstrasse
Bus 100, 157, 348
Unter den Linden 7
Tel. 20 35 40
Mon–Fri 10 a.m.–8 pm.;
Sat, Sun and holidays 2–8 p.m.
On the east side of Bebelplatz, the national opera house (1743) was the first edifice of the Forum Fridericianum, the monumental complex with which Friedrich the Great wanted to express his personal attachment to the arts,

scholarship and religious tolerance. Designed by Georg Wenzelaus von Knobelsdorff in the style of a classical Palladian palazzo, the opera house staged the world premieres of Otto Nicolai's *Merry Wives of Windsor* in 1849 and Alban Berg's *Wozzeck* in 1925.

Alte Bibliothek G 2
U-, S-Bahn Friedrichstrasse
Bus 100, 157, 348
Bebelplatz
Information tel. 20 93 29 46
Opposite the opera house, the graceful curved façade of the old royal library, now serving Humboldt University, was inspired by the baroque wing of the Hofburg Palace in Vienna.
In the middle of Bebelplatz, a monument by Israeli artist Micha Ullman (1995) commemorates the Nazis' infamous book-burning of May 10, 1933, when university students set alight 20,000 works by Jewish and humanist authors such as Freud, Heine, Thomas and Heinrich Mann.

Friedrich the Great Monument G 2
The Hohenzollerns' most illustrious king is honoured in the centre of the avenue with a masterly bronze equestrian statue by Christian Daniel Rauch, erected in 1851.

Some 150 prominent Prussians of the philosopher-soldier's era are portrayed in sculpted relief on the pedestal. Critics note that in keeping with the nationalist and somewhat philistine spirit of the times, pride of place was given to military heroes and statesmen, while the playwright Gotthold Ephraim Lessing and philosopher Immanuel Kant have been relegated to the rear, beneath the horse's tail.

Humboldt University G 2

- S-Bahn Friedrichstrasse
- Bus 100, 157, 348

Berlin's first university (1810) completes the Forum Fridericianum on the north side of Unter den Linden. It was championed by Prussian statesman-scholar Wilhelm von Humboldt and housed in the palace built in 1766 for Friedrich's brother, Prince Heinrich. Illustrious alumni and teachers have included the brothers Grimm, philosophers Hegel and Schopenhauer, and scientists Einstein and Max Planck. Today, the university has nearly 30,000 students.

Neue Wache G 2

- U-/S-Bahn Friedrichstrasse
- Bus 100, 157, 348
- Unter den Linden 4
- Open daily 10 a.m.–6 p.m.

Next to the university, Karl Friedrich Schinkel's Doric-columned guardhouse, built for the Prussian Army in 1818, became a memorial for the Victims of War and the Rule of Force *(Opfer von Krieg und Gewaltherrschaft)* in 1993. The victims' monument in the hall is a controversial bronze *Pietà* of a mother cradling her dead son, based on a 40-cm miniature by sculptor Käthe Kollwitz and clumsily enlarged to four times the original size.

Zeughaus G 2

- U-, S-Bahn Friedrichstrasse
- Unter den Linden 2
- Tel. 20 30 40
- Pei building open daily 10 a.m.– 6 p.m.

Baroque architect Andreas Schlüter provided the basic design for another Prussian Army building, the grand 17th-century arsenal. It is now the home of the German Historical Museum *(Deutsches Historisches Museum)*. To house the collections, which trace the nation's tumultuous past in painting, photographs and film, the modern architect I. M. Pei added a triangular building with an outside glass and steel spiral staircase. The arsenal's inner courtyard is adorned by Schlüter's brilliantly sculpted death-masks of warriors.

Prinzessinenpalais G 2

- U-, S-Bahn Friedrichstrasse
- Bus 100
- Unter den Linden 5
- Tel. 20 26 83

On the south side of the avenue, the Prinzessinnenpalais (or Opernpalais), built in the 18th century for the Prussian princesses, was fancifully reconstructed in 1969. It is joined by bridge to the Kronprinzenpalais (Crown Princes' Palace), also restored and now a German government residence. The Prinzessinnenpalais houses several cafés and restaurants, including the very popular Operncafé and its open-air terrace.

Schlossbrücke G 2

Linking Unter den Linden to what was once the royal palace, the castle bridge is a creation (1824) of Karl Friedrich Schinkel. He also created its bronze reliefs of mythical sea creatures, but his designs for marble statues of military heroes were added later. The bridge joins the "mainland" Unter den Linden to the Spreeinsel island in the middle of the Spree River where the fishermen of Cölln, Berlin's earliest community, had their homes. Their memory is preserved in the name of the Fischerinsel housing development at the south end of the island.

Schlossplatz G 2

Dominating the island, this vast square has been of enormous historical significance in city life. It was here in 1443 that Prince Elector Friedrich II von Hohenzollern built the first fortress. Known simply as the Berliner Schloss, it grew progressively in the 17th century until Andreas Schlüter's great façade, completed in 1706, made it the city's grandest baroque edifice. It was here that the monarch, cheered by crowds on the square, saw his troops off to war in 1870 and again in 1914.

In 1918, revolutionary leader Karl Liebknecht stood on the royal balcony to proclaim a bolshevik-style republic. The castle was gutted by fire in World War II and dismantled in 1951 by the communist East German regime as an unacceptable symbol of "monarchistic autocracy". It was replaced by the bronze-glass, steel and white marble **Palast der Republik**, home of the communist East German rubber-stamp parliament, and has been closed since 1991 because of asbestos poisoning. The royal balcony of the baroque palace was incorporated into the old communist **Staatsratsgebäude** (Council of State) on the south side of the square. In July 2002, the Parliament

decided to rebuilt the façade of the historic castle.

Berliner Dom G 2

- S-Bahn Hackescher Markt
- Bus 100, 157, 200, 348
- Am Lustgarten

With its great dome and four towers looming over the square's northeast corner, this gigantic neo-baroque cathedral was built in 1905 to give Kaiser Wilhelm II a German Protestant rival to St Peter's in Rome. It was to serve as the royal family's church and mausoleum—six Hohenzollerns are buried in the main church and another 94 in the crypt. The bright interior provides a colourful setting for theatre performances and concerts in addition to church services.

Museumsinsel G 2

- S-Bahn Hackescher Markt
- U-, S-Bahn Friedrichstrasse
- Tram 1, 50
- Opening times for all museums:
  Daily (except Mon) 10 a.m.–6 p.m.
  Thurs to 10 p.m.
- Hotline: 20 90 55 55

The northern end of the Spree island was developed as a museum

Treasures of classical antiquity are housed in the Pergamon Museum.

omplex back in 1830, took
00 years to complete and is now
undergoing extensive restoration.
or the moment, only the Altes
Museum, the Pergamon Museum
and the Alte Nationalgalerie are
open to the public. The Neues
Museum, being restored by British
architect David Chipperfield, will
reunite the Egyptian collections of
eastern and western Berlin,
including the famous bust of Queen
Nefertiti currently in Schloss
Charlottenburg's Egyptian Museum.
At the island's northernmost point,
the neo-baroque Bode Museum,
dedicated to the national
museums' most illustrious director,
Wilhelm von Bode, is to exhibit
(end 2005) sculptural collections
and art of the late Roman and
Byzantine eras.

Altes Museum G 2

The oldest museum in Berlin is
Schinkel's masterpiece. It houses
awe-inspiring collections of Greek
and Roman antiquities. The rotunda
is supported by 20 corinthian
columns.

Alte Nationalgalerie G 2

After complete renovation, this
museum displays major 19th-
century works by German
painters such as Schadow, Caspar
David Friedrich, Böcklin, Feuerbach,
Menzel and Lieberman, but also
Cézanne, Manet and Rodin.

Pergamon Museum G 2

The most popular of the island's
museums is named after its main
attraction, the monumental ancient
Greek Pergamon Altar, dating from
the 2nd century BC. The huge
colonnaded marble altar dedicated
to Zeus was excavated and shipped
in sections from Bergama in Turkish
Anatolia to be installed here at the
end of the 19th century. Sculpted
friezes show Greek gods battling
with giants.

In a similar way, archaeologists
have reassembled the grand
Processional Way and Ishtar Gate
(562 BC) of the Babylonian king
Nebuchadnezzar II. It depicts the
lions of the goddess Ishtar striding
along the blue and ochre glazed
brick walls to the gate, which is
adorned with divine bulls and
dragons.

The Roman Market Gateway of
Miletus (120 AD), with its imposing
arches and Ionic and Corinthian
columns, completes the museum's
trio of monumental reconstructions.

Blindes Vertrauen G 1

S-Bahn Hackescher Markt
U-Bahn Oranienburger Tor
Rosenthaler Strasse 39
Sat, Sun 1–7 p.m.

Blind Trust is a poignant museum housed in the workshop where from 1941 to 1943 owner Otto Weidt protected Jewish and non-Jewish blind and deaf-mutes from the Nazi extermination camps.

Neue Synagoge G 1

- S-Bahn Hackescher Markt
- U-Bahn Oranienburger Tor
- Oranienburger Strasse 28/30
- For opening hours tel. 88 02 80

The gilded and glass Moorish-style domes of Germany's grandest synagogue (1866) give the street its landmark. It was protected from the *Kristallnacht* fires of 1938 by a brave Berlin policeman, but an Allied bomb hit it in 1943. The synagogue has been restored as a *Centrum Judaicum* documenting the community's history. Marking the old **Jewish cemetery** on nearby Grosse Hamburger Strasse, razed by the Nazi Gestapo in 1943, is a gravestone for the community's famous 18th-century philosopher, Moses Mendelssohn.

Tacheles – Internationales Kunsthaus G 1

- U-Bahn Oranienburger Tor
- Oranienburger Strasse 54
- Tel. 282 61 85 or 281 61 19

An artists' cooperative in a disused shopping gallery. Community action has preserved it from demolition to make it a multicultural monument at the centre of an arts, commercial and residential complex.

ORANIENBURGER STRASSE F–G 1

Trams and cars vie for space on this busy but relatively narrow shopping street, to which eastern Berlin's reviving Jewish community has returned, sharing the quarter with the more colourful elements of the city's "alternative" counter-culture—and prostitutes. At the corner of Tucholskystrasse, the German Post Office is restoring its splendid 19th-century glazed brick and terracotta **Postfuhramt** (Mail Coach Office). At the east end of Oranienburger Strasse, a monumental *Jugendstil* (Art nouveau) façade beckons to a delightful group of courtyards, the **Hackesche Höfe**, between Rosenthaler- and Sophienstrasse. This classical piece of Berlin urban architecture has added to its orginal apartments and workshops a whole complex of art galleries, studios, restaurants, cafés, cabaret-theatre, cinemas and shops. The neighbourhood to the northeast is still known as **Scheunenviertel** (Barn District), from 17th-century grain storehouses subsequently used as workshops and tenements for Jewish refugees from Poland and Russia.

ALEXANDERPLATZ

"Alex" to Berliners, the immense square has evolved from farmland to cattle market, military parade ground to modern traffic hub, attracting mass demonstrations in 1848, 1918 and again in November 1989—five days before the Wall came down. Today, it is a pedestrian zone around the railway station. Of its office blocks, some are architectural monuments like Peter Behrens' Alexander- and Berolinahaus (1932) on the south side of the square. But others are characterless additions of the 1960s, due for demolition in plans to restore the square's central role in eastern Berlin life with a new group of skyscrapers. East of Alexanderplatz, the apartment buildings of Karl-Marx-Allee offer an intriguing glimpse of how the 1950s Stalinist architecture was given a facelift in the 1990s.

Fernsehturm H 2
- U-, S-Bahn Alexanderplatz
- Tram 2, 3, 4, 5, 6
- Bus 100, 157, 348
- Panoramastrasse 1a
- Tel. 242 33 33
- Observation deck open daily 10 a.m.–midnight
- Telecafé daily 10 a.m.–midnight
- Live music Tues to Sat from 7 p.m.

Beyond Schlossplatz, the avenue that began with the royal Unter den Linden becomes the more proletarian Karl-Liebknecht-Strasse, leading to one of the East German regime's proudest monuments, the 365-m (1,200-ft) Television Tower. The city's tallest structure was inaugurated in 1969 as a bombastic counterpart to western Berlin's somewhat comic metal Funkturm, a 1920s "mini-Eiffel Tower" in Charlottenburg. The giant concrete needle pierces a steel-and-glass sphere two-thirds of the way up, with a café and revolving observation deck from which the view almost makes the whole thing worthwhile.

Marienkirche G 2
- U-, S-Bahn Alexanderplatz
- Tram 2, 3, 4, 5, 6
- Bus 100, 157, 348
- Karl-Liebknecht-Strasse 8
- Tel. 242 44 67
- Mon–Thurs 10 a.m.–4 p.m.;
- Sat, Sun noon–4 p.m.

Standing in dignified if rather forlorn isolation nearby, this slender 13th-century Gothic structure is one of Berlin's oldest parish churches. Its interior has a fine *Totentanz* (Dance of Death) frieze on the north aisle and a marble pulpit (1703) carved by Andreas Schlüter.

Get close up to the Red Town Hall to see the reliefs on the façade, recounting German history up to the 1860s.

Berliner Rathaus H 2

:::: U-, S-Bahn Alexanderplatz
:::: Tram 2, 3, 4, 5, 6
:::: Bus 100, 142, 157, 348
:::: Rathausstrasse
:::: Tel. 90 26 22 73
:::: Mon–Fri 10 a.m.–6 p.m.
:::: Group tours by appointment.

Southwest of the Fernsehturm, the imposing *Rotes Rathaus* (Red Town Hall), earned its popular nickname from its red brick, rather than ideology.

The building, dating from 1869, found a new purpose in 1991 as residence of the city mayor in office.

Nikolaiviertel G 2

One of the more popular urban achievements of the East German authorities was the construction and reconstruction of the city's medieval neighbourhood stretching between the town hall and the Mühlendamm embankment. Picturesque restaurants and wine-bars cluster convivially around the twin-steepled Gothic parish church.

Museum Nikolaikirche G–H 2

:::: U-, S-Bahn Alexanderplatz
:::: Tram 2, 3, 4, 5, 6
:::: Bus 100, 142, 157, 257, 348

Nikolaikirchplatz
Tel. 24 00 21 82
Daily (except Mon)10 a.m.–6 p.m.
Group tours by appointment
The church built in 1230 today houses folklore and historical collections of the Märkisches Museum.

Museum Ephraim-Palais H 2

S-Bahn Alexanderplatz
Tram 2, 3, 4, 5, 6
Bus 100, 142, 157, 257, 348
Poststrasse 16
Tel. 24 00 21 21
Daily (except Mon)10 a.m.–6 p.m.
The 18th-century baroque home of court banker Veitel Heine Ephraim has been converted into a museum displaying fine examples of Biedermeier furniture.

Museum Knoblauchhaus H 2

U-, S-Bahn Alexanderplatz
Tram 5, 6, 15
Bus 100, 142, 157, 257, 348
Poststrasse 23
Tel. 24 00 21 71
Daily (except Mon) 10 a.m.–6 p.m.
The neoclassical bourgeois townhouse, built in the 18th century, has been turned into a museum documenting the cultivated and tasteful Knoblauch family who lived there for 170 years.

Märkisches Museum H 3

U-Bahn Märkisches Museum
Bus 147, 265
Tel. 30 86 60
Am Köllnischen Park 5
Tel. 30 86 60/36 86 62 15
Daily (except Mon) 10 a.m.–6 p.m.
Over on the river's south bank, this regional museum for the folklore and history of Berlin and Brandenburg has a particularly fine collection devoted to the city's theatre.

BIEDERMEIER

No, he wasn't a famous cabinet-maker or furniture designer. The name applies to much of Germany's popular cultural output in the first half of the 19th century—furniture and architecture, painting and poetry, and painted pottery, too. It was made in the image of its customers: stolid, upright and petty bourgeois. It derived from a satirical figure of "Gottfried Biedermeier" in the *Fliegende Blätter* magazine, the pseudonym used jointly by a writer and a doctor. Carl Spitzweg painted the archetypal Biedermeier Man, a scrawny night-capped fellow in bed holding an open umbrella. And now, after a century of derision, the heavy mahogany veneered furniture is fetching highest prices from Berlin's sophisticated antique dealers.

POTSDAMER PLATZ

Potsdamer Platz is back. Fanning out from the old square to the new Marlene-Dietrich-Platz, the area is bustling once more with ultra-modern cinemas, hotels, casino, shopping mall, restaurants, apartments and office blocks.

Potsdamer Platz F 3

From the day the city's first railway station opened here in 1838, what had been a quiet crossroads on the way to Potsdam grew into a sprawling "town within a town", the epicentre of Berlin's metropolitan tumult. Europe's busiest city square in the 1920s—registering more traffic than London's Marble Arch or Paris's Place de la Concorde—became Europe's largest construction site in the 1990s. Renowned architects came from all over the world to fill the vast 48-hectare (120-acre) wasteland left by wartime bombs and the neglect of the Wall years. The main thoroughfare of this new district is Neue Potsdamer Strasse, separating the Daimler-Areal from the Sony Center, and ending at Potsdamer Platz. Italy's Renzo Piano designed the tall **debis-Tower** for the **Quartier Daimler-Chrysler**, topped by a gleaming green cube. Neighbouring buildings were designed by local architect Hans Kollhoff and the Japanese Arata Isozaki. From the top of the Panorama-Punkt, 96 m (118 ft) high, you get a good view of this spectacular urban revival. Chicago's Helmut Jahn built the **Sony entertainment complex** beneath a fibre-glass flat-topped pyramid recalling the Japanese manufacturer's beloved Mount Fuji. Only two buildings survived World War II: **Weinhaus Huth**, now a wine-bar and restaurant hemmed in by new shops, and a façade of the old Esplanade hotel appropriated for apartments in the Sony complex.

Martin-Gropius-Bau F 3

U-, S-Bahn Potsdamer Platz
Bus 129, 248, 341
Tel. 25 48 60/25 48 91 68
Niederkirchnerstrasse 7
Daily (except Mon)
10 a.m.–8 p.m.
Late closing Sat 10 p.m.
This lovingly restored 19th-century building was designed by the great-uncle of Bauhaus master Walter Gropius. It stages first-rate temporary exhibitions of sculpture, paintings, photography and architecture, all with an accent on Berlin's cultural history. It has a pleasant café and bookshop.

Potsdamer Platz, Sony Center: a bright new look for a former wasteland.

Filmmuseum Berlin F 3

U-, S-Bahn Potsdamer Platz
Bus 129, 248, 341
Potsdamerstrasse 2
Daily (except Mon) 10 a.m.–6 p.m.
Late closing Tues 8 p.m.
Tel. 300 90 30

A glimpse into the history of the German film industry, with several rooms devoted to Marlene Dietrich. Library, two cinemas and boutique.

Topographie des Terrors F 3

U-, S-Bahn Potsdamer Platz
Bus 129, 248, 341
Entrance Niederkirchnerstrasse 8, at the Martin-Gropius-Bau
Daily 10 a.m.–6 p.m.;
May–Sept to 8 p.m.
Information tel. 25 48 67 03

The deliberately grim new museum is being built over remains of the Nazi Gestapo headquarters. Until it opens in 2005, an open-air exhibition documents how, in the former Prinz-Albrecht Hotel, Heinrich Himmler's secret police imprisoned, tortured and murdered its political and "racial" enemies.

Anhalter Bahnhof F 4

Askanischer Platz

Further south, another eloquent ruin can be seen, the arcades of the red-brick neo-Renaissance façade of what was once the city's most glamorous railway station. It was from here, after 1933, that some of Germany's most famous people went into exile: Albert Einstein, George Grosz, Heinrich Mann, Bertolt Brecht and Kurt Weill. Designed by Franz Schwechten, the station was closed down and demolished in 1952.

BERLIN WALL

East of the Martin-Gropius-Bau on Niederkirchnerstrasse, you can see the preserved remains of the infamous Wall that divided the city from 1961 to 1989. Elsewhere in town, you may come across red markings in the street where it traced the 45-km (28-mile) border shutting West Berlin off not only from East Berlin but also the East German hinterland. After wholesale destruction, in large part to sell off pieces as souvenirs, other stretches of wall, now protected as historical monuments, are located at Bernauer Strasse and Scharnhorst Strasse in the northern district of Wedding. The longest stretch, 1.3 km (0.8 miles), is now the East-Side-Gallery, in Mühlenstrasse near the Warschauer Strasse U-Bahn station, exhibiting the eloquent artwork and graffiti that were painted—on the west side of the Wall.

Checkpoint Charlie G 3

U-Bahn Kochstrasse

From 1961 to 1989, this was one of the most famous focal points of the Cold War. Between Kochstrasse and Zimmerstrasse, the US Army manned a checkpoint at the border crossing between West and East Berlin. On the other side, East German border guards were delegated by their Soviet masters to control traffic and watch out for fugitives, while customs officials checked papers and personal belongings. Around the customs sheds was a vast floodlit no-man's-land with tank-traps, obstacles to slow down traffic and watchtowers for armed guards. Today, the Friedrichstrasse crossing is marked only by its old sign: "You Are Leaving the American Sector", and two large photos in the middle of the road—a Soviet soldier facing south and an American soldier facing north.

Haus am Checkpoint Charlie G 3

U-Bahn Kochstrasse
Friedrichstrasse 41–45
Tel. 253 72 50
Open daily 9 a.m.–10 p.m.

This small private museum occupies premises of the old Café Kölln, once the crisis HQ for foreign correspondents.

TIERGARTEN

The Tiergarten, a pleasant park, has given its name to the whole neighbourhood between Mitte and Charlottenburg. The "Animal Garden" was a forest where the Hohenzollern kings hunted for deer and wild boar. Today, it is a popular venue for picnics, particularly for Turkish barbecues, and rock concerts and for boating on its ponds. Its trees date only from 1949, all the others having been cut down for fuel in the hard times after World War II. The park is split by the broad, straight Strasse des 17. Juni (date of an East German workers' uprising in 1953). At weekends a flea market and crafts market are held in front of the S-Bahn Tiergarten station. In the southeast of the park is the Kulturforum and its museums of European art.

Philharmonie E 3
: U-, S-Bahn Potsdamer Platz
: Bus 129, 142, 148, 248, 348
: Kulturforum
: Herbert-von-Karajan-Strasse 1
: Tel. enquiries 25 48 80
: Mon–Fri 3–6 p.m.;
: Sat, Sun and holidays
: 11 a.m.–2 p.m.
Hans Scharoun, who masterminded the Kulturforum's original concept, built this tent-like home for the Berlin Philharmonic Orchestra in keeping with his taste for free-form structure. Working closely with the orchestra's legendary dictatorial conductor, Herbert von Karajan, he gave the orchestra awesome acoustics in a space designed for all to see the conductor's baton. The building is flanked by the **Kammermusiksaal** (Chamber Music Hall) and the smaller **Musikinstrumenten-Museum**.

Gemäldegalerie E 3
: U-, S-Bahn Potsdamer Platz
: Bus 129, 142, 148, 248, 348
: Kulturforum
: Matthäikirchplatz 8
: Tel. 26 60/20 90 55 55
: Daily (except Mon) 10 a.m.–6 p.m.
: Late closing Thurs 10 p.m.
At the heart of the Tiergarten's Kulturforum complex of the fine arts, music and libraries, this museum presents one of the world's finest collections of European painting, from the Middle Ages to the 18th century. After 50 years of Cold War separation, the collections from the Museumsinsel in the east and Dahlem in the west have been reunited in this wonderful setting. Superb lighting enhances the paintings. The highlights include German: Schongauer, Altdorfer,

Dürer and Cranach;
Dutch and Flemish: Van Eyck,
Memling, Brueghel, Rubens, Van
Dyck, Rembrandt and Vermeer;
Italian: Giotto, Botticelli, Raphael,
Giorgione and Caravaggio;
French: Georges de la Tour, Poussin
and Watteau; Spanish: Velázquez
and Zurbarán; English: Reynolds
and Gainsborough.
Adjoining is the bulky red-brick
Kunstgewerbemuseum
displaying the Guelf treasury and
Lüneburg silver.

Neue Nationalgalerie E 3

- U-, S-Bahn Potsdamer Platz
- Bus 129, 142, 148, 248, 348
- Kulturforum
- Potsdamer Strasse 50
- Tel. 2 66 26 62/20 90 55 55
- Tues, Wed, Fri 10 a.m.–6 p.m.;
- Thurs 10 a.m.–10 p.m.;
- Sat, Sun 11 a.m.–6 p.m.

The striking black steel and glass
gallery for 20th-century and
contemporary sculpture and
painting is a late work (1968) of
Bauhaus architect Ludwig Mies van
der Rohe, who left Germany in
1937. The gallery stages temporary
exhibitions on the ground floor,
with its permanent collection on

*The Zoo has one of the most varied
collections of animals in Europe.*

the lower level. There are major
works by Edvard Munch, Kokoschka
and Picasso, Kirchner, Schmit-
Rottluff, Grosz, Nolde, Beckmann
and Dix; among Mies's Bauhaus
contemporaries: Klee and
Kandinsky. American art is well
represented by Morris Louis, Stella,
Newman and Rothko. Sculpture on
the outside terrace presents works
by Ernst, Giacometti, Moore,
Picasso, Calder.

St Matthäi-Kirche E 3

- U-, S-Bahn Potsdamer Platz
- Bus 129, 142, 148, 248, 348
- Matthäikirchplatz
- Tel. 262 12 02
- Tues–Sun noon–6 p.m., also
- open for services

The simple little neo-Romanesque
church (1846) behind the Neue
Nationalgalerie stands in piquant
contrast to the forum's modern
architecture. It looks like an
oversight left by Hitler when he
razed all else here to make way for
the first projected monuments for
Germania, the new capital of his
"Thousand-Year Reich".

Bauhaus-Archiv –
Museum für Gestaltung D 3

- Bus 100, 129, 187, 341
- Klingelhöferstrasse 14
- Tel. 254 00 20/254 00 278
- Daily (except Tues) 10 a.m.–5 p.m.

BAHNHOF ZOO

In the years of divided Berlin, this major railway station for trains arriving from western Germany was notorious for the marginal outsiders squatting its entrance halls all day long. Today, its bustling, late-closing shopping centre has transformed the station into a much brighter, more "user-friendly" place, two of its star attractions being the city's biggest international newspaper shop and the stand outside selling what connoisseurs consider to be Germany's best pretzels.

For the archives and exhibition halls of the historic Bauhaus design school, its founder Walter Gropius designed the building completed in 1978, nine years after his death. It houses original Bauhaus furniture, textiles, architectural models, sculpture, paintings and other art works.

Zoologischer Garten C 3

- U-, S-Bahn Zoologischer Garten
- Bus X9, X34, 100, 145, 249
- Hardenbergplatz 8,
- Budapester Strasse 32/34
- Tel. 25 40 10
- Open daily 9 a.m.–6.30 p.m.

The entrance to the zoo, which opened in 1884, is through a pagoda-roofed Elephant Gate.

Animals on view include Indian and African elephants, pandas, rhinoceros and crocodiles.

Siegessäule D 2–3

- Bus 100, 187, 341
- Strasse des 17. Juni
- Am Grossen Stern
- Tel. 391 29 61
- Observation platform daily
- 9.30 a.m.–5.30 p.m.

Soaring above the Grosser Stern traffic circle at the centre of the Tiergarten, this Victory Column celebrates Prussian victories over Denmark in 1864, Austria in 1866 and France in 1871. Beneath the gilded statue of Winged Victory is an observation platform reached by a spiral staircase of 285 steps. The wars' heroes, Chancellor Bismarck, Field Marshal Moltke and War Minister Roon, have their statues on the north side of the traffic circle.

Haus der Kulturen der Welt E 2

- Bus 100
- John-Forster-Dulles-Allee 10
- Tel. 39 78 70
- Exhibitions daily (except Mon)
- noon–6 p.m.

Better known as "the pregnant oyster" (*die schwangere Auster*), the congress hall presents concerts and exhibitions from the world's five

continents. Its pond has a bronze sculpture by Henry Moore.
The 68 bells of the black granite Carillon tower in the Tiergarten opposite chime out at noon and 5 p.m.

Reichstagsgebäude, Deutscher Bundestag F 2

S-Bahn Unter den Linden
Bus 100, 248, 257, 348
Platz der Republik
Tel. 22 73 21 52
Dome open daily 8 a.m.– midnight. For the rest of the building, visits by appointment only.
Roof-garden restaurant by reservation only; tel. 226 29 90; daily 9 a.m.–4.30 p.m.; 6.30 p.m.–midnight.

One of the great achievements of German democracy has been to overcome the sombre image of this massive 19th-century parliamentary building and make it downright popular. Two foreign artists have contributed to the transformation. In 1995, Bulgarian conceptual artist Christo wrapped the building up in fabric like a parcel and attracted 5 million visitors. People were suddenly amused and charmed by the place whose fire in 1933 had enabled Hitler to destroy freedom for 12 years. In 1999, British architect Norman Foster completed its magical glass dome, imparting a new lightness to the whole edifice. And that dome is open to the public, accessible by elevator and spiral ramp to the very top.
The inscription over the Corinthian-columned western portico, *Dem Deutschen Volke* (To the German People) suddenly makes more sense.
Do not miss the new Chancellery, completed in 2001. The office of the Chancellor is in a 9-storey cube, 36 m (118 ft high).

Hamburger Bahnhof— Museum für Gegenwart Berlin D–E 2

S-Bahn Lehrter Stadtbahnhof
Bus 245, 430
Invalidenstrasse 50/51
Tel. 397 83 40/20 90 55 55
Tues, Wed, Fri 10 a.m.–6 p.m.;
Thurs 10 a.m.–10 p.m.;
Sat, Sun 11 a.m.–6 p.m.

Off the beaten track on the north side of the Spree, one of Germany's oldest railway stations (1847) has been converted into a museum of contemporary art. Major exhibits include works by Joseph Beuys, Georg Baselitz, Anselm Kiefer, video artist Nam Jun Paik and, from the US, Andy Warhol, Robert Rauschenberg and Dan Flavin, whose neon lighting also graces the building's façade.

CHARLOTTENBURG

Cutting through the centre of Charlottenburg is the Kurfürstendamm, literally the Prince Elector's Embankment, and commonly known as the Ku'damm. At its eastern end, where it turns into Tauentzienstrasse, it retains an imperial symbol with the Kaiser-Wilhelm-Gedächtniskirche. It extends westwards 3.5 km (2 miles) to the more humble Halensee railway station.

Kaiser-Wilhelm-Gedächtnis-Kirche C 4
: U-, S-Bahn Zoologischer Garten
: Bus 100, 109, 119
: Breitscheidplatz
: Tel. 218 50 23
: Daily 9 a.m.–7 p.m.;
: Sat 9 a.m.–6 p.m., followed by an
: organ recital

The ruin of the Kaiser Wilhelm Memorial Church (1895) and its modern additions are one of Berlin's most important symbols of World War II and peacetime recovery. With characteristic irreverence, Berliners puncture its poignancy by referring to its bomb-smashed spire as the "broken tooth", and the more recent hexagonal belltower and octagonal chapel as the "lipstick" and "powder compact". More serious visitors will appreciate in the neo-Romanesque church the carved reliefs and friezes honouring the Hohenzollern rulers.

Europa-Center C 4
: U-Bahn Kurfürstendamm or
: Wittenbergplatz
: S-Bahn Zoologischer Garten
: Tauentzienstrasse 9–12
: Tel. 348 00 88

Sharing Breitscheidplatz with the Kaiser Wilhelm Memorial Church, this high-rise shopping centre includes a hotel, cinemas and offices. It was a quite conscious proclamation of 1960s consumer capitalism in the Cold War contest with East Berlin. The Mercedes-Benz star was equally explicitly placed on top of its 22-storey tower as an emblem of Western luxury. Down below on the square, people gather around the amiable granite **Weltkugelbrunnen** (Fountain of Planet Earth) without giving too much thought to its symbolism.

KaDeWe D 4
: U-Bahn Wittenbergplatz
: Tauentzienstrasse 21–24
: Tel. 212 10
: Mon–Fri 9.30 a.m.–8 p.m.,
: Sat 9 a.m.–6 p.m.

Located not far from the Ku'damm along Tauentzienstrasse, this most opulent of department stores bears as its full name Kaufhaus des Westens (Department Store of the West), its totally unideological title since it was opened in 1907. Nonetheless, its most memorable day in recent years was November 10, 1989, the morning after the Wall came down. Even if most East Berliners could not afford its French and Italian designer clothes and the mind-boggling array of exotic delicacies in the food halls, this was the place where they wanted to see what they had been missing for all those years.

Jüdische Gemeinde zu Berlin (Gemeindehaus) C 4

U-Bahn Uhlandstrasse
or Kurfürstenstrasse
S-Bahn Zoologischer Garten
Fasanenstrasse 79
Tel. 88 02 80

North of the Ku'damm, set back on a courtyard, the Jewish Community Centre is a modern building that has incorporated as its entrance the domed portal of the synagogue destroyed by the Nazis on *Kristallnacht* (Crystal Night), November 9, 1938. Apart from the

Embracing but not quite touching: Berlin sculpture symbolizes in steel the divided city.

synagogue, the centre has a small library which is open to the general public.

Käthe Kollwitz Museum C 4

- U-Bahn Uhlandstrasse
  or Kurfürstendamm
- S-Bahn Zoologischer Garten
  Fasanenstrasse 24
  Tel. 882 52 10
- Daily (except Tues) 11 a.m.–6 p.m.

Housed in an elegant villa, this small museum displays sketches and sculptures by Kollwitz (1867–1945). Born in Königsberg, she studied in Berlin and married a doctor who worked in a poor area of the city. Her home and studio in Prenzlauer Berg were destroyed by bombs in 1943.

Savignyplatz B 3–4

- S-Bahn Savignyplatz
- Bus 149

Beyond the arches of the rather forbidding elevated railway, this tree-shaded square and its three offshoots—Carmer-, Knesebeck- and Grolmannstrasse—are frequented by numerous artists, writers, actors and their groupies. The area is full of bookshops, art galleries, gourmet restaurants and grungy-chic bars.

KURFÜRSTENDAMM A 5–C 5

This bright and breezy avenue enjoyed two heydays in the 20th century. In the Golden Twenties, it was the hub of the city's elegant new theatre, restaurant and shopping area, the *Neuer Westen* (New West) competing with the established pomp of Unter den Linden and the more brassy flair of Friedrichstrasse. In the Cold War years, it was the showcase street of West Berlin and in 1989 the first place East Berliners made for when the Wall came down. Today, it has to compete with the revival of eastern Berlin, but its essence of bourgeois chic is still there in the smart boutiques, theatres, cinemas and cafés.

Like its rival, Unter den Linden, the Ku'damm had started as part of a bridle path, between the city centre and the royal hunting lodge in Grunewald forest. Bismarck came back after the Prussians' 1871 victory in Paris determined to turn it into a Champs-Elysées.

Fashionable landmarks along the way include the **Kempinski Hotel**, where people who can't afford a room splash out on a drink at the grand Bristol Bar. At the west end of the avenue, the **Schaubühne** avant-garde theatre is part of Erich Mendelssohn's 1920s "Woga" complex, revolutionary for its time in combining in one building cinema, cabaret, shops, hotel and apartments.

The fauna here may remind you of the colourful characters satirized by Berlin painter George Grosz in the 1920s. Upon his return from exile in the United States in 1959, he made one last round of the bars before dying at Savignyplatz 6.

The Story of Berlin B 4

- U-Bahn Uhlandstrasse or Kurfürstendamm
- S-Bahn Savignyplatz
- Bus X9, X10, 100, 109, 119, 129, 219, 249
- Kurfürstendamm 207–208
- Tel. 887 20 100
- Open daily 10 a.m.–8 p.m., last entry 6 p.m.

A state-of-the art multimedia display documenting the history of Berlin, from its foundation in 1237 to the present day. Guided tours are given in 12 languages. A time tunnel, a series of "event rooms" and 3-D sound systems take you back into the past.

Particularly impressive is the anti-atomic bunker, built deep down beneath ground level, which gives you the weird feeling of reliving the Cold War.

Schloss Charlottenburg A 2

- Bus X21, 109, 145, 210
- Luisenplatz
- Tel. 32 09 11
- Daily (except Mon) 10 a.m.–5 p.m.

Queen Sophie Charlotte's summer residence was begun on an intimate scale in 1695 and grew by the 18th century into one of Prussia's finest baroque edifices. Johann Friedrich Eosander designed the lofty dome and the west wing's Orangerie, while Georg von Knobelsdorff added the comely east wing for Friedrich the Great. Originally commissioned for the Berliner Schloss, Andreas Schlüter's bronze equestrian statue of Friedrich-Wilhelm (1697) ended up in the courtyard here in 1952. It had to be rescued from Tegel lake

FASANENSTRASSE C 4

The Ku'damm's shopping area includes a distinctive set of cross-streets: Meineke-, Uhland-, Knesebeck-, Bleibtreu- and, most elegant of all, Fasanenstrasse. Here you will find a number of fine restaurants, art and antique galleries, fashionable boutiques, luxury shopping arcades and courtyards. Many of them are housed in handsome mansions of the prosperous *Gründerzeit* (Founding Years) of 19th-century Germany. The Wintergarten Ensemble south of the Ku'damm includes the Literaturhaus, with bookshop and a delightful garden-restaurant, and the Käthe Kollwitz Museum devoted to the life and work of the 20th-century sculptor.

Schloss Charlottenburg developed from a small summer residence into a fully fledged palace.

after it sank with a barge fleeing World War II bombardment. Interior furnishings destroyed in the war have been replaced by pieces taken from other baroque Prussian palaces. In the Royal Apartments, the major attractions are the **Porzellankabinett** of Japanese and Chinese porcelain from the 17th and 18th centuries, the richly decorated **Eosanderkapelle** (Eosander Chapel) and the **Eichengalerie** (Oak Gallery), the exquisite setting then and now for chamber music recitals.

The majority of the palace's magnificent art collection is housed on the first floor of the east wing, most notably the eight French masterpieces by Watteau in the **Goldene Galerie** ballroom, named for its decorative gilded stucco.

The palace **gardens**, one of the Berliners' favourite green spaces, combine formal French and "natural" English landscaping. The pretty Italian-style Schinkel-Pavillon was added near the entrance to the east wing in 1824. Royal porcelain from the Königliche Porzellan-Manufaktur is displayed in the baroque **Belvedere** north of the carp pond.

Ägyptisches Museum & Papyrussammlung A 2

- U-Bahn Sophie-Charlotte Platz
- Bus X21, 109, 145, 210
- Schlossstrasse 70
- Tel. 343 57 30
- Daily (except Mon)10 a.m.–6 p.m.

Opposite the Schloss, pending transfer to the Museumsinsel (planned for 2007), Berlin's collection of over 2,000 pieces of ancient Egyptian sculpture, jewellery, ceramics and papyrus includes the world-famous bust of Queen Nefertiti (1340 BC) with its original colours untouched, and a small head of a man known as the Berlin Green Head. From Egypt's Roman era, the monumental Kalabsha Gate (20 BC) shows Emperor Augustus in carved relief as a pharaoh making sacred offerings to Egyptian deities.

Sammlung Berggruen A 2

- Bus X21, 109, 145, 210
- Schlossstrasse 1
- Tel. 326 95 80 or 20 90 55 55
- Tues–Fri 10 a.m.–6 p.m.;
- Sat, Sun 11 a.m.–6 p.m.

In this museum created in 1996 from the collection of Heinz Berggruen, the emphasis is on Picasso and his contemporaries. Over 70 paintings and sculptures trace the Spanish master's career, alongside works by Van Gogh, Cézanne, Braque, Klee and Giacometti. The collection is constantly expanding.

Bröhan Museum A 2

- U-Bahn Richard-Wagner-Platz
- Bus X21, 109, 145, 210
- Schlossstrasse 1a
- Tel. 32 69 06 00
- Daily (except Mon)10 a.m.–6 p.m.

The Karl Bröhan collection—the gift of a merchant from Hamburg—presents all the artistic tendencies between 1889 and 1939 Jugendstil (Art Nouveau) and Art Deco furniture, silverware, porcelain, glassware and sculpture, with paintings by Max Liebermann and Lovis Corinth.

Olympiastadion off map by A 1

- U-, S-Bahn Olympiastadion
- Bus A 18, 149
- Olympischer Platz

In the area known as Westend, Hitler had this sports stadium built for the 1936 Berlin Olympics, to accommodate 100,000 spectators. Earmarked as the British Army post-war headquarters, it was spared Allied bombs. Until 1990, parades celebrated Queen Elizabeth's birthday where once Nazi storm troopers saluted Hitler. The stadium is now the home of Hertha Berlin football club and can seat 76,000 spectators.

OUTLYING DISTRICTS

To see the easy-going, cosmopolitan side of the city, explore eastern Berlin's old working-class district of Prenzlauer Berg, traditionally shortened to Prenz'lberg, northeast of Mitte. Or venture into Kreuzberg, south of Mitte, home to the largest Turkish community outside Turkey.

Prenzlauer Berg off map by H 1
⋮ U-Bahn Schönhauser Allee
Buildings on and around **Schönhauser Allee**, the main thoroughfare of Prenzlauer Berg, have been largely "gentrified" since the fall of the Wall. Landmarks here include the **Jüdischer Friedhof** (Jewish Cemetery) at N° 23–25, last resting place of painter Max Liebermann, composer Giacomo Meyerbeer and publisher Leopold Ullstein. The **Kultur-Brauerei** at N° 36–39 is a grand old red-brick brewery converted into an arts complex for cinema, theatre, exhibitions and exhibitionist "happenings" (entrance on Knaackstrasse). Further north, a few paces along Stargarder Strasse, **Gethsemane-Kirche** was a rallying point for "revolutionary" activity in 1989 aiming to transform the GDR, and often the scene of open fights with the police.

Kollwitzplatz, a square named after sculptor Käthe Kollwitz and her doctor husband Karl, has rapidly become a more easy-going but just as fashionable counterpart to western Berlin's Savignyplatz. Open-air café terraces and Italian, Alsatian and Russian restaurants lend the quarter a new cosmopolitan air. Galleries and artists' studios are mushrooming in its side streets.

Eastern Berlin's main **synagogue** is at nearby Rykestrasse 53 in a rear courtyard, this one preserved from fire in 1938 because adjacent apartments belong to Nazi party officials.

Kreuzberg F–H 3–6
The neighbourhood takes its name from the hill in **Viktoria Park** (F 6, U-Bahn Platz der Luftbrücke) topped by Karl Friedrich Schinkel's neo-Gothic Nationaldenkmal (National Monument) and cascade to commemorate Germany's defeat of Napoleon. There's an adventure park here for the kids, and a beergarden and restaurant with dance floor.

In the 1970s and 80s, the neglected tenement buildings of the part of Kreuzberg north of the Landwehr canal, bordered by the Wall, were taken over by western Berlin's largest communities of quatters, punks and Turks. The area s still full of cafés, bars and clubs, and remains the centre of gay Berlin, but it has sobered up quite a ot since the Wall came down.

Oranienstrasse, a bustling thoroughfare (G–H 4, U-Bahn Moritzplatz), brings together Kreuzberg's Turkish and "alternative" communities of artists and students. Junk shops, health-food stores, New Age emporiums and all-night bars peacefully coexist with Turkish groceries, restaurants and Anatolian travel agents.

Turkish Market off map by H 6

U-Bahn Kottbusser Tor
Maybachufer
Tues, Fri noon–6.30 p.m.

The two banks of the canal illustrate perfectly the development of the Kreuzberg district over the last quarter of a century. The noisy, crowded market spreading along the south bank displays all the spices, fruit, fish, exotic fabrics, carpets and household goods typical of any bazaar in Istanbul or Anatolia. Along the north bank of the canal, Paul-Lincke-Ufer, fashionable cafés and boutiques beneath elegant balconied apartments have been installed in *Jugendstil* (Art Nouveau) buildings, restored as part of the district's post-Wall gentrification.

Jüdisches Museum G 4

U-Bahn Hallesches Tor
Bus 129
Lindenstrasse 9–14, Kreuzberg
Tel. 25 99 33 00
Daily 10 a.m.–8 p.m.;
Monday late closing 10 p.m.

Daniel Libeskind's astonishing design makes Berlin's new Jewish Museum an experience in itself. Austere, eloquent and powerful, it is for many the ultimate monument to Jewish life in Germany— interlocking its glory and its tragedy. Incorporating a handsome baroque Prussian courthouse of 1735, to which it is linked by an underground passage, an elongated zigzagging concrete building forms a dislocated Star of David. Narrow windows are slashed in its tall grey walls like knife wounds.

The old courthouse is reserved for temporary shows, films, recitals and conferences. The new museum's permanent exhibits trace with art and artefacts, photographs and documents the rich and proud Berlin Jewish story, integrated architecturally with the climactic fact of the Holocaust. Every staircase, every sloping corridor, dimly or brightly lit room, even the sound of a heavy grating door closing sharply behind the visitor, has an existential resonance.

EXCURSIONS

For rest and recreation, Berliners have no lack of greenery, with lakes, beaches and shady woodland within easy reach by train or bus.

Spandau
- U-Bahn Zitadelle,
- Altstadt or Rathaus

Northwest of Berlin, this ancient borough remains a country village a world apart from the metropolis. At Breite Strasse 32, the oldest house boasts a 15th-century Gothic vaulted interior. On Markstrasse and Ritterstrasse are other noteworthy houses, with fine 17th- and 18th-century gables and arches. The Gothic Nikolaikirche dates back to the 15th century, but the belfry is largely baroque and its altar 16th-century Renaissance. Prince Elector Joachim II is honoured with a bronze statue here for having bowed to the citizens' pressure to adopt their Protestant faith in 1539.

Stadtgeschichtliches Museum Spandau
- U-Bahn Zitadelle
- Bus 133
- Am Juliusturm
- Tel. 354 94 42 00
- Tues–Fri 9 a.m.–5 p.m.; Sat, Sun and holidays 10 a.m.–5 p.m.

The museum devoted to the history of the town is housed in the 16th-century red-brick Citadel, embracing the older medieval Juliusturm (Julius Tower).

Dahlem Museums
- U-Bahn to Dahlem-Dorf
- For opening times
- tel. 8 30 11 or 8 39 01

During the years of the city's division, this group of museums southwest of the centre was the main focus of West Berlin's art collections. They have undergone extensive restructuring.

The **Ethnologische Museum**, devoted to early art and artefacts of the Americas, Africa, Asia, the Pacific islands and non-German-speaking Europe, was the first to reopen. Then followed the **Museum für Indische Kunst** (Indian Art) and **für Ostasiatische Kunst** (East Asian Art).

Brücke-Museum
- S-Bahn Zehlendorf
- Bus 115
- Bussardsteig 9, Zehlendorf
- Tel 8 31 20 29
- Daily (except Tues) 11 a.m.–5 p.m.

This fine little museum draws on a comprehensive collection of early 20th-century German Expressionist painters working in Dresden under the name *Die Brücke* (The Bridge, as

a symbol of their group solidarity): Kirchner, Nolde, Heckel and Schmidt-Rottluff.

Haus der Wannseekonferenz

- S-Bahn Wannsee
- Bus 114
- Am Grossen Wannsee 56–58, Zehlendorf
- Tel. 805 00 10
- Open daily 10 a.m.–6 p.m.

The Wannsee Conference House is an elegant bourgeois villa where top Nazis made formal plans to execute Hitler's order for the extermination of Europe's Jews. Now a museum, its documents, photographs and film relate the 1942 conference, chaired by SS leader Reinhard Heydrich, and the results as organized by Adolf Eichmann, also present.

Grunewald

- S-Bahn Grunewald

The forests and lakes of Grunewald southwest of the city have always provided Berliners with their most convenient recreation area, 32 sq km (12 sq miles). Never was this more vital than when West Berlin was cut off from the outside world by the Wall. Vast stretches of pine trees have been supplemented by handsome groves of chestnut, oak, birch, beech and lime, providing a protected habitat for wild boar, deer, foxes and rabbits. The shores of Wannsee, Krumme Lanke and Schlachtensee welcome bathers to sandy beaches complete with old-fashioned sheltered basket-seats.

Pfaueninsel

Take a ferry across the Havel River to Peacock Island, a nature reserve with soaring lodgepole pines, venerable oaks and a bird sanctuary. Among the English landscaped gardens are a romantic (but fake) castle ruin and Schinkel's charming Schweizer Haus (Swiss Cottage).

Potsdam

- S-Bahn Potsdam Hauptbahnhof
- 40 minutes by road or rail from the city centre

The capital of Brandenburg lies at the southwest corner of Berlin. In a delightful setting of royal palaces surrounded by parks and lakes, it displays a largely graceful facet of Prussia's history. The garrison town that the Sergeant King Friedrich-Wilhelm I created in the 18th century was transformed by his more sophisticated son, Friedrich the Great, into a haven for the arts and refinements of a more courtly life. The city's dominant feature is still today Sanssouci Palace, which he lovingly turned into a German

...ersailles. Under the Nazis, the town returned to its militaristic beginnings, with Hitler receiving the "blessing" of Field Marshal Hindenburg at the Garnisonkirche (destroyed after the war). Hitler's conquerors closed this chapter by meeting in Potsdam to divide up defeated Germany.

In 1991, the coffins of the two kings were brought back to be buried at Sanssouci—Friedrich the Great on the palace terrace and his not exactly beloved father some distance away in the Friedenskirche.

Schloss Sanssouci

Tram 94, 98
Bus 612, 692, 695
Maulbeerallee, Potsdam
Tel. (0331) 96 94 190
Guided tours only, daily (except Mon) 9 a.m.–4 p.m.

Friedrich the Great built himself a palace where he could pursue his tastes for music, art and philosophy without a worry—*sans souci*—about the affairs of state. Architect Georg von Knobelsdorff drew on the king's own sketches to create in 1745 an exquisite rococo residence forming a harmonious whole with its terraced vine-covered gardens. In the lovely Konzertzimmer, a 19th-century painting by Adolf von Menzel shows how Friedrich played flute there to the harpsichord of Carl Philip Emmanuel Bach, son of Johann Sebastian. The king kept his personal library of over 2,000 French books in the cedarwood Bibliothek of the east wing rotunda. French was also the language of his "philosophical suppers", held in the central Marmorsaal (Marble Hall) and animated by Voltaire from 1750 to 1753.

The palace gardens, in formal French design and landscaped English style, cover some 300 hectares. Friedrich's **Bildergalerie** (Picture Gallery) east of the palace includes Flemish and Italian works by Van Dyck, Rubens, Caravaggio and Guido Reni. You are free to visit without a guide.

Southwest of the terraced gardens, the **Chinesisches Teehaus** boasts gilded palm trees and a gilded mandarin on its pagoda roof.

The immense **Neue Palais**, at the western end of the main avenue, was built by Frederick II after the Seven Years' War, as a symbol of Prussian might.

Altstadt

Potsdam's Old Town area is still recovering from bombardments of 1945 and the later dismantling of Hohenzollern monuments by the East German communist government. On Alter Markt, Karl

In the 19th century Friedrich-Wilhelm IV added an Italianate Orangerie to the gardens of Sanssouci Palace.

Friedrich Schinkel's neoclassical Nikolai-Kirche with its gigantic dome has been restored; it dominates the charming but more modest silhouette of the rebuilt 18th-century Altes Rathaus (Old Town Hall). The Knobelsdorff-Haus (1750), nearby, is named after its architect. Of the Hohenzollerns' Stadtschloss (Town Palace) only the 17th-century Marstall remains, royal stables now converted to house the Film Museum and cinematheque.

The main feature of old Potsdam is its shopping street, Brandenburger Strasse, lined with several 18th-century houses. It leads to the triumphal arch of the Brandenburg Gate (1779), preceding its famous Berlin counterpart by 10 years.

Holländisches Viertel

On and around Mittelstrasse is the Dutch Quarter: one of the few aesthetic initiatives of the Sergeant King Friedrich-Wilhelm I. These handsome red-brick houses were built from 1734 to 1740 as homes for Dutch craftsmen. Most of them left and were replaced by an artists colony, but their 128 houses form one of the region's most pleasant neighbourhoods. Many of the houses conceal delightful garden-taverns in their inner courtyards. The market on Bassinplatz offers an impressive array of local produce. Brandenburg vegetables and fruit are among the best in Germany, particularly the asparagus, apples, cherries and strawberries.

Kolonie Alexandrowka

Potsdam's other "foreign" quarter is this self-contained Russian village created on the north side of town by Friedrich-Wilhelm III for veterans of the Napoleonic Wars, in honour of Tsar Alexander I. Descendants still live in the typical timbered datchas and worship at the onion-domed Russian Orthodox Alexander Nevski Chapel.

Schloss Cecilienhof

Bus 694
Tel. (0331) 96 94 244
Open daily 9 a.m.–4 p.m.
Joseph Stalin, Harry Truman and Winston Churchill met in this 19th-century English-style country manor to negotiate the Potsdam Treaty that carved up Germany in 1945. The house has been preserved as a museum. Among the documents in the conference rooms is an accreditation as press photographer for John Fitzgerald Kennedy, who wangled his way in as son of the American ambassador.

Babelsberg Studiotour

S-Bahn Griebnitzsee,
then bus 693
August-Babel-Strasse 26–53
Information tel. 0331 721 27 55
Reservation tel. 0331 721 27 59
Guided tours from mid March to early November
In summer you can visit the old UFA Studios of Germany's cinema era of the 1920s and 30s. Special effects and children's TV shows form part of the attractions.

Köpenick

S-Bahn Köpenick
Southeast of Berlin, the historic centre of the borough of Köpenick is built on an island at the confluence of the Spree river and the Dahme tributary.
Schloss Köpenick (17th century) is currently under restoration, and from 2004 will function as a museum of interior decoration (Museum der Raumkunst). The most handsome dwellings of the old town (18th century) are on the Alter Markt and Alt-Köpenick street. The splendid red-brick neo-Gothic town hall (built 1901–03) boasts an imposing courtyard and monumental staircase.
Since reunification, Köpenick's lake, **Grosser Müggelsee**, has regained its popularity for water sports, sailing and fishing.

Dining Out

Berlin has restaurants for every taste and for every wallet, and you can eat your way around the world. The German answer to nouvelle cuisine is *neue deutsche Küche*, traditional German dishes prepared in a lighter, more imaginative manner. Our selection of restaurants follows the same order as the sightseeing chapters in this guide, and an indication of prices for a typical meal is indicated by € signs:

€ = under 17 euro

€€ = 17–32 euro

€€€ = 32–55 euro

€€€€ = over 55 euro

UNTER DEN LINDEN

Adlon
S-Bahn Unter den Linden
Unter den Linden 77
Tel. 22 61 15 55
Daily 6.30 a.m.–11.30 p.m.
Berlin's most exclusive restaurant. French and German cuisine. €€€€

Aigner
U-Bahn Hausvogteiplatz, Französische Strasse
Französische Strasse 25
Tel. 203 75 18 50
Daily noon–1 a.m.
Regional cuisine with an Austrian accent; the classics are duck Brandenburger style, and *Tafelspitz*, boiled beef. €€

Borchardt
U 6 Französische Strasse
Französische Strasse 47
Tel. 20 38 71 10
Daily 11.30 a.m.–1 a.m.
Elegant restaurant. Its grand dining room with marble columns is a meeting place for Berlin's political and cultural celebrities. €€€

Cafe Einstein
S-Bahn Unter den Linden
Unter den Linden 42
Tel. 422 04 36 32
Daily 10 a.m.–2 a.m.
Austrian café. In summer, the garden is the place to be seen. €

Cibo Matto
U-Bahn Weinmeisterstrasse
S-Bahn Hackescher Markt
Rosenthaler Strasse 44
Tel. 28 38 51 70
Daily 9 a.m.–3 a.m.
(Fri and Sat closes later)
Italian cuisine in a friendly, welcoming atmosphere. €

Dressler

- S-Bahn Unter den Linden
- Unter den Linden 39
- Tel. 204 44 22
- Daily 8 a.m.–1 a.m.

Art Deco setting, reminiscent of the 1920s and 30s. €€

Die Eins

- S-Bahn Friedrichstrasse or
- Unter den Linden
- Wilhelmstrasse 67a
- Tel. 22 48 98 88
- Mon–Sat from 9 a.m.,
- Sun from 10 a.m.

Bar/restaurant on the banks of the Spree, not far from the Brandenburg Gate in the heart of the new government district. The terrace looks onto the Reichstag. €€

Fridas Schwester

- U-Bahn Weinmeisterstrasse
- S-Bahn Hackescher Markt
- Neue Schönhauser Strasse 11
- Tel. 28 38 47 10
- Daily from 10 a.m.;
- Fri, Sat to 3 a.m.

Cosmopolitan cuisine: specialities from Austria, Italy, Mexico and California. €€

Der Kartoffelkeller

- U-Bahn Friedrichstrasse
- Albrechtstrasse 14b
- Tel. 282 85 48
- Daily 11 a.m.–1 a.m.
- Reservation recommended.

The potato is king in this restaurant where the humble tuber is transformed into all kinds of

---

A GERMAN MENU

Typical starters include *Hackepeter*, the German version of steak tartare, and *Soleier*, eggs pickled in brine, then peeled, halved and seasoned with salt, pepper, paprika, vinegar and oil. They are usually eaten with Berlin mustard, *Mostrich*.

Fish comes fresh from the Havel. Try specialities such as *Havelaal grün*, eel in dill sauce, or *Havelzander*, pikeperch, with *Salzkartoffeln*—simple but tasty boiled potatoes. In fact, potatoes are something of a Berlin obsession: one of the city's gourmet delights is the *Kartoffelpuffer*, a crispy potato pancake, often accompanied by *Äpfelmus*—apple sauce.

If you have a hearty appetite and no vegetarian tendencies, tackle the supreme Berlin delicacy *Eisbein mit Sauerkraut und Erbsenpüree*—pig's knuckle on a purée of peas with *sauerkraut*.

A popular sweet is *Rote Grütze* (a compote of raspberries, cherries and blackcurrants). Otherwise, Berliners happily tuck into a generous slice of *Schwarzwälder Kirschtorte*, the creamy layered cherry and chocolate gateau from the Black Forest.

gourmet dishes, many taken from very old cookbooks. €

Las Cucarachas
- U-Bahn Oranienburger Tor
- S-Bahn Oranienburger Strasse
- Oranienburger Strasse 38
- Tel. 282 20 44
- Daily noon–2 a.m.
- Mon–Fri lunch menu under 10€

Mexican restaurant and bar with summer terrace. €

Newton Bar
- U-Bahn Französische Strasse
- Charlottenstrasse 57
- Tel. 2029 54 21
- Daily from 10 a.m.

Cool and trendy, attracting a cosmopolitan clientele who come for the superb cocktails. The walls are hung with photos by Helmut Newton. Cigar-smokers will be impressed by Berlin's biggest humidor on the first floor. €€€

Operncafé
- U-Bahn Hausvogteiplatz
- Bus 100
- Unter den Linden 5
- Tel. 20 26 86
- Café open daily 9 a.m.–midnight
- Restaurant open daily
- noon–midnight

Berlin's biggest coffee house, with more than 50 different cakes and gateaux on the menu. €€

Oren
- S-Bahn Oranienburger Strasse
- U-Bahn Oranienburger Tor
- Tram 13
- Oranienburger Strasse 28
- Tel. 282 82 28
- Mon–Sat 10 a.m.–2 a.m.;
- Sun 10 a.m.–1 a.m.

Jewish cuisine and vegetarian dishes, with a lot of fish. €€

Oxymoron
- S-Bahn Hackescher Markt
- Rosenthaler Strasse 40,
- Main entrance on Hackesche Höfe
- Tel. 28 39 18 86
- Daily from 11 a.m.;
- Thurs–Sat club from 11 p.m.;
- Wed from 7 p.m. after-work party

International atmosphere; a unique mix of restaurant, salon, club and café. €€

Schwarzenraben
- U-Bahn Weinmeisterstrasse or
- Rosa–Luxemburg-Platz
- Neue Schönhauser Strasse 13
- Tel. 50 57 55 33
- Daily 10 a.m.–4 a.m.

Mediterranean cuisine with an Italian accent. €€

Ständige Vertretung
- S-Bahn Friedrichstrasse
- Schiffbauerdamm 8
- Tel. 282 39 65
- Daily 11 a.m.–2 a.m.

Cologne and its famous Kölsch-Bier brought to Berlin. €

Yosoy

- U-Bahn Weinmeisterstrasse
- Rosenthaler Strasse 37
- Tel. 28 39 12 13
- Daily from 11 a.m.

Enormous choice of tapas and Rioja served from the barrel. The seafood platter for two is well worth investigating. All ingredients flown in fresh from Spain. €

ALEXANDERPLATZ

Brazil

- U-Bahn Weinmeisterstrasse
- Gormannstrasse 22
- Tel. 28 59 90 26
- Daily from 10 a.m.;
- Mon "happy day"

Brazilian food and an intriguing atmosphere. €

Cafe Hu

- S-Bahn Alexanderplatz
- Karl-Liebknecht-Strasse 9
- Tel. 241 57 15
- Mon–Fri 3–10 p.m.;
- Sat, Sun 2–10 p.m.

Elegant café with Hungarian atmosphere on Alexanderplatz. €

Mutter Hoppe

- S-Bahn Alexanderplatz
- Rathausstrasse 21
- Tel. 24 72 06 03
- Daily 11.30 a.m.–1 a.m.

Meat is high on the list of priorities of this restaurant proposing good German cuisine and live music at the weekend. €

Reinhard's Biergarten

- U-, S-Bahn Alexanderplatz
- Tram Alexanderplatz
- Poststrasse 28
- Tel. 242 52 95
- Daily 9 a.m.–1 a.m.

In heart of the historic Nikolai district, a restaurant with a hint of 1920s atmosphere, serving seasonal German cuisine. €

Restauration Tucholsky

- U-Bahn Torstrasse
- Torstrasse 189
- Tel. 281 73 49
- Mon–Fri noon–midnight;
- Sat, Sun to 1 a.m.

Cosy German restaurant and plenty of documentation on Tucholsky. €€

Tele-Café Fernsehturm

- S-Bahn Alexanderplatz
- Tram Alexanderplatz
- Panoramastrasse 1a
- Tel. 242 33 33
- Daily 9 a.m.–1 a.m.

German cuisine to set your head spinning. The café turns a full circle in 30 minutes, providing a sensational panorama. €

DRINKS

The top German wines are considered to be the Riesling wines of the Rheingau. But Berlin's most popular drink remains beer. It is served *vom Fass*, on tap, or bottled, in these varieties: Export, light and smooth; Pils, light and very dry; and Bock, dark and rich. You will see Berliners drinking a red or green liquid from large bowl-like glasses: that's *Berliner Weisse*, a very pale beer with a shot of raspberry *(mit Rot)* or woodruff syrup *(mit Grün)*.

Zum Nussbaum

- S-Bahn Alexanderplatz
- Am Nussbaum 3
- Tel. 242 30 95
- Daily from noon

This is the oldest restaurant in Berlin, founded in 1571 when the city was still called Cölln. It was destroyed in World War II but has been faithfully reconstructed down to the last detail. The satirical artist Rudolf Heinrich Zille stayed here. €

Zur Letzten Instanz

- S-Bahn Alexanderplatz
- U-Bahn Klosterstrasse
- Waisenstrasse 14–16
- Tel. 242 55 28
- Mon–Sat noon–1 a.m.;
- Sun noon–11 p.m.

Another claimant to the title of oldest establishment in Berlin, this typical pub offers good local cuisine. €

POTSDAMER PLATZ

Diekmann im Weinhaus Huth

- U-/S-Bahn Potsdamer Platz
- Alte Potsdamer Strasse 5
- Tel. 25 29 75 24
- Daily noon–1 a.m.

Enjoy German, French, Italian or Austrian specialities on two terraces overlooking busy Potsdamer Platz. €

Französischer Hof

- U-Bahn Stadtmitte
- Jägerstrasse 56
- Tel. 20 17 71 70
- Daily noon–1 a.m.;
- Sat from 8 p.m.

Cabaret 1920s style. International specialities and a vast choice of excellent wines, directly on the Gendarmenmarkt. €€€

Harry's New York Bar

- U-Bahn Nollendorfplatz
- S-Bahn Potsdamer Platz
- Lützowufer 15 in Hotel Esplanade
- Tel. 25 47 88 21
- Daily from noon
- Mon–Sat live music

One of the most beautiful hotel bars in Berlin, lively until the early hours. €€€

Meistersaal

U-, S-Bahn Potsdamer Platz
Köthener Strasse 38
Tel. 264 95 30
Mon, Tues, Thurs, Sat
6 p.m.–1 a.m.; Fri 6 p.m.–4 a.m.

This is the only building on Potsdamer Platz remaining from 1913. Top-class modern German cuisine. €€

TIERGARTEN

Ambrosius

U–Bahn Kurfürstenstrasse or Nollendorfplatz
Bus 100
Einemstrasse 14 on the corner of Kurfürstenstrasse
Tel. 264 05 26
Mon–Fri 8 a.m.–midnight,
Sat, Sun from 10 a.m.

The menu features 60 specialities and all of them are German. €

Angkor Wat

S-Bahn Bellevue
Bus 187
Paulstrasse 22
Tel. 393 39 22
Daily 6 p.m.–midnight

Inexpensive Khmer cooking: try the Cambodian fondue. €

Bar am Lützowplatz

U-Bahn Nollendorfplatz
Lützowplatz 7
Tel. 25 46 42 66
Daily 2 p.m.–4 a.m.

A classic among Berlin's many cocktail bars, this was chosen as the best in Germany in 1994. More than 140 types of champagne to tickle your tastebuds. €

Cäpt'n Schillow

S-Bahn Zoologischer Garten
Strasse des 17. Juni/
Am Charlottenburger Tor
Tel. 31 50 50 15
Mon to Fri 11 a.m.–11 p.m.;
Sat, Sun 10 a.m.–11 p.m.

Restaurant on a barge on the Landwehr canal. Fish dishes, both local and international recipes. €

Hugo's Restaurant

U-Bahn Wittenbergplatz
S-Bahn Zoologischer Garten
Hotel Intercontinental
Budapester Strasse 2
Tel. 26 02 12 63
Mon to Sat 6 p.m.–midnight

French cuisine in an extremely chic setting, and by far the best foie gras in the city. €€€€

Paris–Moskau

S-Bahn Lehrter Bahnhof/
Hauptbahnhof
Alt-Moabit 141

Tel. 394 20 81

Daily 6 p.m.–1 a.m.

Take a detour up to the working-class district of Moabit for a great culinary experience: excellent fish and seafood dishes, and more than 250 wines in this small half-timbered building dating from 1898, near the railway line linking Paris and Moscow. €

Weinwirtschaft

U-Bahn Hansaplatz

S-Bahn Bellevue

S-Bahnbogen Bellevue

Tel. 39 90 51 56

Mon to Fri 4 p.m.–midnight;

Sat, Sun 2 p.m.–midnight

A wine restaurant with over 20 open wines mainly from German vineyards, and an extensive variety of bottled wine in a wide price range. Simple brick vaults and rustic tables. €

CHARLOTTENBURG

Alcatraz

U-Bahn Richard-Wagner-Platz

Charlottenburger Ufer 1

Tel. 348 24 06

Daily from noon

People are happy to do time in this Mexican restaurant. The food is excellent, the atmosphere irresistible, and there are more than 90 cocktails to whet your appetite. €

Biscotti

U-Bahn Wilmersdorfer Strasse

Pestalozzistrasse 88

Tel. 312 39 37

Mon–Fri 6 p.m.–0.30 a.m.;

Sat from 9.30 a.m.

Mamma mia! Handmade pasta, a small but exquisite selection of high-quality Italian dishes. €€

Bovril

U-Bahn Adenauerplatz

Kurfürstendamm 184

Tel. 881 84 61

Mon–Sat 10 a.m.–2 p.m.

Don't be put off by the name. This is a Ku'damm classic, a meeting place for artists and media folk, and starlets on the first rungs of the ladder to fame. Traditional bistro with frequently changing menu. €€

Carpe Diem

S-Bahn Savignyplatz

Savignypassage/Jeanne-Mammen-Bogen 576/77

Tel. 313 27 28

Daily 2 p.m.–1 a.m.

Delicious tapas to nibble while you linger over the imaginative menus. Excellent cocktails. As it's beneath a railway arch, you hear the trains rumbling overhead. €€

Dicker Wirt

S-Bahn Westend

Danckelmannstrasse 43

You'll need loose-fitting clothes if you want to do justice to a typical Berlin meal.

Tel. 321 99 42
Mon–Sat from noon;
Sun from 10 a.m.
A typical Berlin pub. €

Don Quijote
S-Bahn Savignyplatz
Bleibtreustrasse 41
Tel. 881 32 08
Daily 4 p.m.–1 a.m.
For years this has been the leading Spanish restaurant in Berlin. Olé! €

Florian
U-Bahn Ernst-Reuter-Platz
Bus 149
Grolmannstrasse 52

Tel. 313 91 84
Daily 6 p.m.–3 a.m.
Southern German specialities, refined by a French influence. €

Ho Lin Wah
U-Bahn Zoologischer Garten
Kurfürstendamm 218
Tel. 882 11 71
Daily noon–midnight
Chinese restaurant in the passage, serving delicious dim sum specialities. €

Kashmir Palace
U-Bahn Wittenbergplatz
Bus 119, 129

Marburger Strasse 14
Tel. 214 28 40
Mon 5.30 p.m.–midnight;
Tues–Sun 11.30 a.m.–midnight
Dishes fit for a maharaja, prepared from old recipes used in the royal houses of India. The vegetarian and tandoori specialities are particularly scrumptious. €

Marjellchen
U-Bahn Uhlandstrasse or Adenauerplatz
Mommsenstrasse 9
Tel. 883 26 76
Mon–Sat 5 p.m.–midnight
Even the *New York Times* has praised this restaurant which cooks to recipes handed down by the owner's East Prussian grandmother. Hearty dishes include *Königsberger Klopse* (meatballs of beef and pork with sardines and anchovies) and *Elchbraten* (roast venison). Afterwards you'll need a glass of Danziger Goldwasser (a clear, spicy spirit full of flittering flakes of gold) to get back to your feet. €€

Mar y Sol
S-Bahn Savignyplatz
Savignyplatz 5
Tel. 313 25 93
Daily 11.30 a.m.–2 a.m.
Chic retaurant with a lovely summer terrace; Spanish dishes, excellent, varied *tapas* buffet. €€

Meineke X
U-Bahn Kurfürstendamm
Meinekestrasse 10
Tel. 882 31 58
Daily 10 a.m.–2 a.m.
Café, restaurant and bistro where you can indulge in one of Berlin's best buffets and round off the meal with an old-fashioned schnaps. €€

Sachiko Sushi
U-Bahn Uhlandstrasse
S-Bahn Savignyplatz
Bus 149
Grolmanstrasse 47
Tel. 313 22 82
Daily noon–midnight
Popular sushi bar. Its Japanese name Sachicko means Child of Fortune. €

Wellenstein
U-Bahn Uhlandstrasse
Kurfürstendamm 190
Tel. 881 78 50
Daily 9 a.m.–3 a.m.
Classic music and red velvet create a dreamy atmosphere and a perfect setting for the excellent venison stew with red cabbage. €€

Woolloomooloo
U-Bahn Deutsche Oper or Richard-Wagner-Platz
Röntgenstrasse 7
Tel. 34 70 27 77
Daily 5 p.m.–1 a.m.

Dining Out

Exotic Australian cuisine featuring crocodile, emu and kangaroo steaks. €€

OUTLYING DISTRICTS

Chagall
⋮ U-Bahn Senefelder Platz
Kollwitzstrasse 2
Prenzlauer Berg
Tel. 441 58 81
⋮ Daily 10 a.m.–2 a.m.
A cosy café serving Russian specialities; there's a fireplace and sometimes live music. €

Collins
⋮ U-Bahn Senefelder Platz or Eberswalder Strasse
Sredzkistrasse 28
Tel. 442 25 78
⋮ Daily 6 p.m.–1 a.m.
American bar and restaurant amidst the theatres of Prenzlauer Berg. Steaks, salads, tacos, and a huge cocktail menu. Happy hour 4–8 p.m., blue hour 11 p.m.–1 a.m. Beer garden. €

Frida Kahlo
⋮ U-Bahn Eberswalder Strasse
Tram 13
Lychener Strasse 37
Prenzlauer Berg
Tel. 445 70 16
⋮ Daily 10 a.m.–2 a.m.;
happy hours 6–9 p.m.

Mexican specialities served in hearty portions. Several Mexican beers and tequilas. €

Jelängerjelieber
⋮ S-Bahn Prenzlauer Allee
Göhrener Strasse 1
Prenzlauer Berg
Tel. 441 22 95
⋮ Daily (except Mon) 6 p.m.–2 a.m.
Reputed chefs lay on a creative cuisine of a high standard. €

Konnopkes Imbiß
⋮ U-Bahn Eberswalder Strasse
Directly beneath the U-Bahn
Prenzlauer Berg
Mon–Fri 5 a.m.–7 p.m.;
⋮ Sat, Sun 6 a.m.–6 p.m.
Snack bar serving the best curry sausage (Currywurst) in Berlin. €

Offenbachstuben
⋮ U-Bahn Eberswalder Strasse
Stubbenkammerstrasse 8
Prenzlauer Berg
Tel. 445 85 02
⋮ Daily from 6 p.m.
Carefully prepared French and German cuisine in four beautiful little dining rooms. Highly reputed even before Reunification. €

Ostwind
⋮ Tram Husemannstrasse
Husemannstrasse 13
⋮ Prenzlauer Berg

Tel. 441 59 51
Mon–Sat 6 p.m.–1 a.m.;
Sun 10 a.m.–1 a.m.
The East Wind brings authentic
Chinese cuisine. €

Pasternak

U-Bahn Senefelder Platz
Knaackstrasse 22–24
Prenzlauer Berg
Tel. 441 33 99
Daily 10 a.m.–2 a.m.
Russian specialities in this
renowned literary café. Tuesdays
and Thursdays are "Russian
Romance" days. €

Prater Gaststätte &
Biergarten

U-Bahn Eberswalder Strasse
Tram 13, 53
Kastanienallee 7–9
Prenzlauer Berg
Tel. 448 56 88
Restaurant Mon–Fri 6 p.m.–
2 a.m.; Sat, Sun 2 p.m.–3 a.m.;
Biergarten Mon–Fri 4 p.m.–
midnight; Sat, Sun noon–midnight
Berlin's oldest and loveliest
beergarden, with regional
specialities and a clientele of
actors, artists and locals. €

Trattoria Paparazzi

U-Bahn Eberswalder Strasse
Tram 1, 20
Husemannstrasse 35

Prenzlauer Berg
Tel. 440 73 33
Daily 6 p.m.–0.30 a.m.
Italian institution, where the locals
and businessmen get together.
Fresh food and a good choice of
wines. €€

Weitzmann

U-Bahn Senefelder Platz
Tram Husemannstrasse
Husemannstrasse 2
Prenzlauer Berg
Tel. 442 71 25
Daily 9 a.m.–1 a.m.
The city's one and only Bauhaus-
style restaurant. Seasonal
specialities from Berlin and
Brandenburg, moderately priced. €

Joe Penas

U-Bahn Gneisenaustrasse
Marheinekeplatz 3
Kreuzberg
Tel. 693 60 44
Daily from 5 p.m.
Trendy place with exuberant décor
and Mexican cuisine. €€

Matto

U-Bahn Platz der Luftbrücke
Bus 119 Kreuzbergstrasse
Chamissoplatz 4
Kreuzberg
Tel. 691 40 21
Mon–Fri from 8 p.m.;
Sat, Sun 10 a.m.–2 a.m.

The taste of Switzerland: *Züri Geschnetzeltes* (sliced veal and mushrooms in cream sauce), *röstis* with bacon and salad, and home-made pasta. €€

Sale e Tabacchi
U-Bahn Stadtmitte or Kochstrasse
Kochstrasse 18, Kreuzberg
Tel. 25 29 50 03
Daily 9 a.m.–1 a.m.;
Sat, Sun 10 a.m.–1 a.m.
The best of Bella Italia in the publishing district. €

Shima
U-Bahn Eisenacher Strasse
Schwäbische Strasse 5
Schöneberg
Tel. 211 19 90
Daily from 6 p.m.
Very stylish restaurant with laid-back lounge area; Asian cuisine. €€

Storch
U-Bahn Eisenacher Strasse
Wartburgstrasse 54
Schöneberg
Tel. 784 20 59
Daily 6 p.m.–1 a.m.
The menu changes daily, but there's always *Flammenkuchen* (savoury tart with very thin crust) and a fine selection of wines. €

Bleibtreu 31
U-Bahn Uhlandstrasse
Bleibtreustr. 31
Wilmersdorf
Tel. 88 47 40
Open all day and all night.
Breakfast from 6 a.m.
New German cuisine and regional specialities such as game stew with fresh mushrooms, broccoli with almonds and home-made *spätzle* (vaguely like tiny dumplings). The menu changes every month. €€

Scarabeo
U-Bahn Hohenzollernplatz
S-Bahn Savignyplatz
Ludwigkirchstrasse 6
Wilmersdorf
Tel. 885 06 16
Mon to Fri 4 p.m.–1 a.m.;
Sat, Sun 4 p.m.–3 a.m.
Restaurant, bar, gallery and library. Here you can savour delectable Egyptian specialities, fine teas and traditional pastries that no pharaoh would disdain. €€€

South Africa
U-Bahn Adenauerplatz
Bus 119, 219
Kurfürstendamm 72
Wilmersdorf
Tel. 32 70 70 55
Daily from 2 p.m.
For a change, how about stewed rattlesnake, saddle of kudu, ostrich steaks or zebra ham, and 150 different South African wines. €€

Entertainment

They say that Berlin never closes. For news of what's on, see *Tip* and *Zitty,* lively magazines appearing every two weeks, or the Time Out website: www.timeout.com/berlin

For theatre and musical events, book in advance through Berlin Tourismus Marketing, tel. 25 00 25, the KaDeWe department store, tel. 217 77 54, or try for last-minute discounts through Hekticket, Hardenbergstr. 29d (Bahnhof Zoo), or Karl-Liebknecht-Strasse 12 (Alexanderplatz), tel. 230 99 30.

CLASSICAL MUSIC

Berlin's long musical tradition attracts the world's finest performers to its grand concert halls, while three main opera houses maintain the city's reputation. Church music can be heard at the Berliner Dom and St Hedwig's Catholic cathedral.

Philharmonie E 3
U-, S-Bahn Potsdamer Platz
Bus 129, 142, 148, 248, 348
Kulturforum
Herbert-von-Karajan-Strasse 1
Information Tel. 25 40 80
Box office 25 48 81 32
Mon–Fri 3–6 p.m.; Sat, Sun and holidays 11 a.m.–2 p.m.
The home of the Berlin Philharmonic Orchestra. The **Kammermusiksaal**, next door, holds regular chamber music and solo recitals (same phone numer).

Konzerthaus Berlin G 3
U-Bahn Stadtmitte or
Französische Str.
S-Bahn Friedrichstr.
Bus 142, 147, 257, 348
Gendarmenmarkt
Box office 203 09 21 01/02
Mon–Sat noon–7 p.m.; Sun and holidays noon–4 p.m.
In the former Schauspielhaus, the Konzerthaus Berlin has a large concert hall and smaller one for chamber music.

Deutsche Oper B 3
U-Bahn Bismarckstrasse
Bus 101, 109
Bismarckstr. 35
Information tel. 343 84 01
Tickets tel. 0700 67 37 23 75 46
International repertoire, usually rendered in the original text.

Deutsche Staatsoper G 2
U-Bahn Friedrichstrasse or Hausvogteiplatz
S-Bahn Friedrichstrasse
Bus 100, 157, 348

Unter den Linden 7
Box office 20 35 45 55
Mon–Fri 11 a.m.–8 p.m.
Daniel Barenboim has been musical and artistic director of the municipal opera house since 1992. International operas in a splendid setting.

Komische Oper F 2

S-Bahn Unter den Linden
Bus 101, 109
Behrenstr. 55–57
Tel. 20 26 06 66
Information tel. 20 26 06 66
Tickets tel. 47 99 74 00 or
018 05 30 41 68

The Comic Opera specializes in presenting operas in their German versions.

MUSICAL COMEDY AND VARIETY

Berlin can claim to have invented the musical comedy before the Americans made it their own—often with the talents of Berlin exiles like Kurt Weill. Today, it is still going strong.

Theater des Westens C 3

U-, S-Bahn Zoologischer Garten
Kantstr. 12
Information tel. 882 28 88
Tickets tel. 018 05 99 89 99

Musicals written by Germans and old Broadway musicals staged in German.

Theater am Potsdamer Platz F 3

U-Bahn Mendelssohn-Bartholdy-Park
S-Bahn Potsdamer Platz
Bus 142, 143
Marlene-Dietrich-Platz 1
Tel. 018 05 114 113

FriedrichstadtPalast F 1

U-Bahn Oranienburger Tor
Friedrichstr. 107
Tel. 23 26 23 26
Box office Tues–Sat 10 a.m.–
8 p.m.; Sun, Mon 10 a.m.–6 p.m.

THEATRE

The public theatre fights its ongoing battle with budget-cutters, but great classical and experimental drama still has a solid home in Berlin.

Friends of Italian Opera G 6

U-Bahn Platz der Luftbrücke
Fidicinstrasse 40
Tel. 693 56 92
www.thefriends.de

If you're hankering to see a play in English, this is the place for you. The theatre was founded in 1990 and hosts visiting companies.

Berliner Ensemble F 2

U-, S-Bahn Friedrichstrasse
Bus 147, 157, Tram 1, 50
Bertolt-Brecht-Platz 1
Tel. 28 40 81 55

Deutsches Theater/ Kammerspiele F 1
- U-, S-Bahn Friedrichstrasse
- Bus 147, 157, Tram 1, 50
- Schumannstr. 13
- Tel. 284 41 222/225

Komödie B 4
- U-Bahn Uhlandstrasse
- Bus 119, 129
- Kurfürstendamm 206–209
- Information tel. 47 99 74 40
- Tickets tel. 88 59 11 88

Renaissance-Theater B 3
- U-Bahn Ernst-Reuter-Platz
- Bus X9, 145, 245
- Hardenbergstr. 6
- Tel. 312 42 02

Schaubühne A 4
- U-Bahn Adenauerplatz
- Bus 110, 119, 129, 219
- Kurfürstendamm 153
- Tel. 89 00 23

Volksbühne H 1
- U-Bahn Rosa-Luxemburg-Platz
- Rosa-Luxemburg-Platz
- Tel. 247 67 72 or 247 76 94

CINEMA

Non-German films are sometimes shown in original versions on the Ku' damm, Potsdamer Platz or in Kreuzberg art-house cinemas. The great annual event is the Berlin Film Festival in February on Potsdamer Platz, where tickets are available.

CABARET

Being naturally irreverent, caustic and witty, Berliners have made satirical cabaret, particularly of the political variety, their own art form. After a period of stagnation, the targets of its satirical barbs are back in town with the national government moving from Bonn to Berlin in 1999. Cabaret's golden era was the 1920s. The Schall und Rauch (Noise and Smoke) club in Max Reinhardt's Grosses Schauspielhaus theatre attracted Berlin's top creative talents. Photomontage artist John Heartfield and painter George Grosz designed the programme. Political commentator Kurt Tucholsky collaborated with poets Klabund and Walter Mehring to write mordant songs and sketches. Star singers included Claire Waldoff, Marlene Dietrich and Trude Hesterberg, the latter using an unknown fellow named Bert Brecht to write her songs. Today, the clubs to look out for are **Bar Jeder Vernunft** (Beyond All Reason), Schaperstr. 24, tel. 883 15 82; **Distel**, Friedrichstr. 101, tel. 204 47 04; **Die Stachelschweine** (Porcupines), in the Europa-Center, tel. 261 47 95; and **Die Wühlmäuse** (Voles), Nürnberger Str. 33, tel. 80 60 29 29.

The Hard Facts

To plan your trip, here are some of the practical details you should know about Berlin:

Airports
Berlin has three airports, all sharing the same phone number: 01805 00 01 86.

Tegel Airport, just north of Charlottenburg, only 8 km (5 miles) from the city centre, is the busiest. The JetExpressBus Line TXL shuttles between the airport and Mitte. Buses X9 and 109 go to the Bahnhof Zoo, and there is a shuttle to U-Bahn station Jakob-Kaiser-Platz, line 7. The airport has a tourist information office in the main terminal, open daily 5 a.m.–10.30 p.m.

Schönefeld, in eastern Berlin, 22 km (14 miles) from the city centre, is undergoing expansion to become the city's principal airport. The fastest public transport into the city centre is by SXL bus to U-Bahn station Rudow, line 7; or the S-Bahn line 9 via Alexanderplatz to Bahnhof Zoo.

Tempelhof, in what was the American Sector, 6 km (4 miles) from the city centre, handles mainly charter and domestic flights. Take bus 119 to the Ku'damm, or U-Bahn line 9 direction Friedrichstrasse.

Climate
Berlin has a healthy continental climate well known among Germans for the bracing quality of its air. Winters are crisp and cold, with the city's lakes and canals often freezing over for New Year's Day skating parties. Summers are warm, at times very hot, but not humid and so never stifling. Westerly winds bring showers in spring and autumn, but they rarely last long.

Despite the pollution common to every modern metropolis, Berlin's prevailing bright clear light gives its blue skies a pellucid quality of fine porcelain.

Clothing
Berlin's continental climate demands really warm clothing outside the spring and summer seasons, and a sweater (for cool evenings) and rainwear all year round. Otherwise, clothing should be light—in summer, cottons are less sticky than synthetics. Good walking shoes are important for excursions around the woods and lakes.

Communications

Call worldwide with telecards from street-phones, much cheaper than the hotel's surcharge service. International dialling code to Germany is 49, and Berlin's city code is 30.

Post your letters and postcards for countries outside Germany in the slot marked *Andere Richtungen*. The Joachimsthaler Strasse post office (Bahnhof Zoo/Kaufhaus Karstadt) is open Mon–Sat 8 a.m.–midnight; the post office in the S-Bahn station Friedrichstrasse opens daily 8 a.m.–10 p.m. You can send e-mails and faxes from here.

Customs Controls

These are minimal at point of entry. Residents of European Union countries may import a reasonable quantity of goods for personal use bought or acquired inside the EU but not at a duty-free shop. People from outside the EU are entitled to a duty-free allowance of 200 cigarettes or 100 cigarillos or 50 cigars or 250 g of tobacco, 1 litre of spirits (exceeding 22%) and 2 litres of distilled beverages (less than 22%) and 2 litres of wine.

Driving

Berlin suffers from the same traffic snarls as any other European metropolis, but it does have good Autobahns and broad straight highways to get you fast to the outlying suburbs, woods and lakes. Parking in the city centre is a real problem, so keep your car only for longer trips.

Seat-belts are compulsory, and children under 12 must sit in the back of the car. Speed limits: motorway 130 kph (80 mph); country highways 100 kph (60 mph) and in town 50 kph (30 mph). Some sections of the motorway may have lower limits: watch out for the signs. Parking in town is permitted only in marked zones. Lead-free petrol is *bleifrei*.

Emergencies

Telephone numbers for police 110, fire brigade 112. Consular help is there only for critical situations, lost passports or worse, not for lost cash or travel tickets.

Formalities

At your port of entry, a valid passport is all that most of you will need—just an identity card for members of EC countries. No special health certificates are required for European or North American citizens.

Health

Residents of EU countries should obtain an E111 form from their local post office before leaving home, in order to benefit from the reciprocal health agreement. (The form will be replaced by a European Health Card by end 2005). Doctors, dentists and hospital staff are of generally good standard, many speaking English. If you anticipate need of prescription medicines, take your own as you may not find the exact equivalent on the spot.

Languages

Many but by no means all Germans speak some English, particularly the younger generation. Like any other "natives", Germans will be pleasantly surprised to hear you greet them with a couple of words in their language. A *Guten Tag* (good morning) or *Guten Abend* (good evening), *Bitte* (please), *Danke* (thanks), *Bitte schön* (don't mention it) and *Auf Wiedersehen* are always welcome.

Media

British and other European newspapers, the *International Herald Tribune* and European edition of the *Wall Street Journal* arrive on the date of publication. Short-wave enthusiasts can tune into BBC World Service, Voice of America and Radio France Internationale. Hotels have cable and satellite TV with several English and American programmes.

Money

The Euro, divided into 100 cents. Coins: 1, 2, 5, 10, 20 and 50 cents, 1 and 2 euros; banknotes: 5, 10, 20, 50, 100, 200 and 500 euros.

Opening Hours

German banks open weekdays 9 a.m.–1 p.m. and 2.30–4 p.m., until 6.30 p.m. on Thursday.

Shops open weekdays 9 a.m.–6.30 p.m. or later, Saturdays 9 a.m.–4 to 8 p.m. (new opening hours are gradually being introduced).

For museums, check with the local tourist office.

Photography

Film for video or still-cameras is of course readily available everywhere. Most museums allow you to use cameras, but ask permission first.

Public Holidays

Jan 1	*Neujahr (*New Year)
May 1	*Tag der Arbeit* (Labour Day)
Oct 3	*Tag der Einheit* (Reunification Day)
Dec 25–26	*Weihnachten* (Christmas)

Moveable:
Christi Himmelfahrt (Ascension Day)
Pfingstmontag (Whit Monday)

Karfreitag (Good Friday)
Ostermontag (Easter Monday)
Buss- und Bettag (Prayer and Repentance Day), third Wednesday in November

Public Transport

The city's BVG network has a fast and efficient service of buses and city trains—subway (U-Bahn) and elevated (S-Bahn). Get maps, information and special tourist tickets in the BVG office at Bahnhof Zoo. Telephone information: 19449, round the clock. See also www.bvg.de

Tickets. The WelcomeCard, 19 euro (June 2002) for one adult and three children, gives three-day unlimited access to all Berlin and Potsdam buses and trains within the city limits, as well as discounts of up to 50 per cent on several special tourist attractions. Other tickets, available from automatic machines or ticket offices, include a single ticket valid for two hours, or weekly tickets, all interchangeable on all BVG buses and trains. Children under age six travel free, under 14 at a reduced rate.

Trains. U-Bahn trains run every three to four minutes, till midnight (1 a.m. at weekends, with all-night weekend service on lines 2, 5, 6, 7, 8, 9, 12 and 15). S-Bahn trains run about every ten minutes.

Buses. Mostly double-decker, with frequent service and good late-night buses on main cross-town routes.

Security

Pickpockets may be active in crowded buses and trains. Without undue paranoia, don't tempt them with an open handbag or a wallet in the hip pocket. Leave passports and valuables in the hotel safe. Bahnhof Zoo still attracts some unsavoury characters, and at night it is best to avoid the U-Bahn and S-Bahn stations at Friedrichstrasse and Alexanderplatz.

Tipping

Service is included in restaurant and hotel bills, shared among the whole staff, but an extra 5 or 10 per cent is customary.

Toilets

The women's room is usually signposted *Damen* and the men's *Herren*. Public toilets are usually immaculate, but if you use the facilities in a bar or restaurant, it is customary to order at least a drink there.

Voltage

Electric current is 220-volt 50-cycle A.C., but take adaptors for any sensitive electronic equipment.

GENERAL EDITOR
  Barbara Ender-Jones
EDITOR
  Christina Grisewood
RESEARCH
  Roland Winter
  and Eckehard Fahldieck
PHOTO CREDITS
  Imagefrance.com
  –/Guglio: inside front cover,
    pp. 8, 59;
  –/Borgese: pp. 1, 28;
  –/Lescourret: p. 42;
  R. Balzerek: p. 31;
  Bildagentur Huber: pp. 2, 5;
  –/Gräfenhain: pp. 13, 24;
  –/R. Schmid: pp. 20, 34, 39;
  –/Damm: pp. 50
MAPS
  Huber Kartographie

Copyright © 2003, 2000
by JPM Publications S.A.
12, avenue William-Fraisse,
1006 Lausanne, Switzerland
E-mail:
information@jpmguides.com
Web site:
http://www.jpmguides.com/

Printed in Switzerland
Weber/Bienne (CTP) — 03/06/01
Edition 2003–2004